# Our Discovery Island

6

T0386014

# STUDENT BOOK

## Future Island

John Wiltshier • José Luis Morales
Series Advisor: David Nunan

Series Consultants:
Hilda Martínez • Xóchitl Arvizu

Advisory Board:
Tim Budden • Tina Chen • Betty Deng
Aaron Jolly • Dr. Nam-Joon Kang • Dr. Wonkey Lee
Wenxin Liang • Ann Mayeda • Wade O. Nichols
Jamie Zhang

**Pearson Education Limited**
Edinburgh Gate
Harlow
Essex CM20 2JE
England
and Associated Companies throughout the world.

Our Discovery Island ™

www.ourdiscoveryisland.com

© Pearson Education Limited 2012

**The *Our Discovery Island* series is an independent educational course published by Pearson Education Limited and is not affiliated with, or authorized, sponsored, or otherwise approved by Discovery Communications LLC or Discovery Education, Inc.**

**The rights of John Wiltshier, José Luis Morales, and Linnette Ansel Erocak to be identified as authors of this work have been asserted by them in accordance with the Copyright, Designs and Patents Act 1988.**

**Stories on pages 6–7, 18, 30, 42, 54, 66, 78, 90, and 102 by Steve Elsworth and Jim Rose. The rights of Steve Elsworth and Jim Rose to be identified as authors of this work have been asserted by them in accordance with the Copyright, Designs and Patents Act 1988.**

First published 2012
Thirteenth impression 2022

ISBN: 978-1-4479-0066-5

Set in Longman English 12.5/15pt
Printed in China (GCC/13)

**Illustrators:** Leo Cultura, Mark Draisey, Michael Garton (The Bright Agency), John Haslam, Ned Jolliffe (Eye Candy Illustration), Simone Massoni (Advocate Art), Moira Millman, Ken Mok, Rui Ricardo (Folio Art), and Olimpia Wong

**Picture Credits:** The publisher would like to thank the following for their kind permission to reproduce their photographs: (Key: b-bottom; c-centre; l-left; r-right; t-top) **Alamy Images:** amana images inc 95b, Arco Images GmbH 29b, Jon Arnold Images Ltd 70tr, ASP GeoImaging / NASA 101cr, Simon Attrill 23tr, Thomas Cockrem 22l, 71b, Emilio Ereza 46cl, Andrew Fox 41 (c), Oliver Gerhard 28r, Images & Stories 101tl, Arif Iqball 94tr, Juice Images 94bl, Paul King 48 (a), Keith Levit 29c, NASA 86, Barrie Neil 17r, Photocuisine 48 (b), Chris Rout 70bl, Christian Schallert 41 (b), Alex Segre 48 (d), David Sutherland 71t, Ken Welsh 46tr; **Art Directors and TRIP Photo Library:** Martin Barlow 95t, Tibor Bognar 101tr, NASA 89 (a), Robin Smith 41 (e), Peter Treanor 47t; **Camera Press Ltd:** Martin Pope 17l; **Corbis:** Quentin Bargate / Loop Images 41 (d), Bettmann 89 (b), 89 (e), 89 (f), Blend Images / Ariel Skelley 62 (e), Cultura 88, Kevin Dodge 47b, Eye Ubiquitous / David Batterbury 62 (g), Image Source 38bc, Juice

Images 40t, Reuters / Stephen Hird 53c, 53b, Sygma / Jacques Haillot 70tl; **FLPA Images of Nature:** Oliver Lucanus / Minden Pictures 29t; **Getty Images:** AFP 53t, Axiom Photographic Agency / Ian Cumming 65tr, Jupiterimages 94br, Science & Society Picture Library 89 (d), The Image Bank / Shannon Fagan 46bl, UpperCut Images / Zave Smith 22cr; **iStockphoto:** Fabio Filzi 101tc, Eric Isselée 24 (b), 24 (e), Valerii Kaliuzhnyi 24 (a), Denis Radovanovic 52 (b), sololos 89 (c), Sawayasu Tsuji 28l; **Pearson Education Ltd:** Jon Barlow 55, Tudor Photography 12 (c), (d); **Photolibrary.com:** age fotostock 52 (a), Nonstock 52 (c), Onoky 65tl; **Rex Features:** Patrick Frilet 23tl, Robert Harding 101br, Jennifer Jacquemart 46tl, Tony Larkin 94tl, Robert Harding / J Lightfoot 40b, Stock Connection / Bill Stevenson 22tr; **Shutterstock.com:** 1000 Words 36tr, 41 (a), Adisa 48 (g), Africa Studio 62 (a), Senai Aksoy 33r (1), aleks.k 91 (1), Anatoli 26 (c), Martin Anderson 87 (3b), Galyna Andrushko 19tr, Andy Dean Photography 52b, Benis Arapovic 62 (h), Yuri Arcurs 80, Atlaspix 60 (g), Evgeniy Ayupov 26 (e), Pierre-Yves Babelon 33l (1), Arvind Balaraman 70cl, Diego Barucco 91 (5), Nick Biemans 33r (4), blinow61 91 (3), Alex James Bramwell 24 (i), Cardiae 26 (g), Rich Carey 33c (5), Matthew Cole 12 (f), Computer Earth 24 (f), 26 (d), Devi 62 (b), Dhoxax 64tl, Dusan964 26 (i), Eddtoro 106tl, Christopher Elwell 24 (g), Enshpil 74 (b), Melinda Fawver 19 (insect repellent), Fivespots 26 (b), Robert Ford 62 (d), Filip Fuxa 87 (4b), Gallimaufry 33l (6), Gelpi 43, Eric Gevaert 33l (3), Mandy Godbehear 67l, Godrick 87 (1b), Goldenangel 87 (2a), Racheal Grazias 60 (b), Anthony Hall 19 (first aid kit), haveseen 60 (d), Mark Herreid 12 (a), Tom Hirtreiter 87 (3a), iofoto 65bl, Eric Isselée 10 (a), 24 (c), 24 (h), 26 (h), J and S Photography 19 (stove), JHDT Stock Images LLC 79, K-i-T 19 (sunblock), Anan Kaewkhammul 33l (4), Kayros Studio 106br, Bill Kennedy 33l (5), Christian Kieffer 64r, Anne Kitzman 62 (c), Kletr 26 (a), Kokhanchikov 12 (e), Veniamin Kraskov 12 (b), F. Krause 74 (c), Tamara Kulikova 19tc, Lalito 74 (f), James Laurie 33c (6), Zastol`skiy Victor Leonidovich 87 (4a), Robyn Mackenzie 74 (a), Viktar Malyshchyts 10 (c), Maska 38tr, Cristi Matei 91 (4), Mikhail 74 (e), Miles Away Photography 33r (6), Karam Miri 19 (pasta), Monkey Business Images 48 (i), Brett Mulcahy 48 (h), Naluwan 10t, Cloudia Newland 87 (2b), NREY 24 (d), John Orsbun 64bl, Pandapaw 24 (j), Losevsky Pavel 38br, Jose Antonio Perez 106bl, Perig 36br, Thomas M Perkins 91bl, Richard Peterson 26 (f), Loo Joo Pheng 33r (2), Kenneth V. Pilon 36tl, PixAchi 64cl, Noel Powell, Schaumburg 91 (2), Jason Prince 33c (4), Prism68 36bc, RDTMOR 10 (b), Restyler 19 (batteries), RM 33r (5), Micha Rosenwirth 87 (1a), Julián Rovagnati 38tl, Elena Schweitzer 10 (d), 74 (d), Joao Seabra 60 (e), SharonPhoto 36tc, Andrea Skjold 48 (f), Dmitry Skutin 74 (g), Stargazer 19 (water), Igor Stevanovic 19 (cans), Alexey Stiop 60 (f), Sukpaiboonwat 19tl, Konstantin Sutyagin 106tr, Tororo Reaction 60 (a), Abel Tumik 19 (matches), Tupungato 60 (c), Ungor 38bl, Vaklav 33r (3), Rui Vale de Sousa 51, Beth Van Trees 67r, Francois van Heerden 33l (2), VAV 19 (flashlight), Dmitry Vereshchagin 74 (h), Tracy Whiteside 23cl, Brad Wynnyk 91br, yxm2008 38tc, Jerry Zitterman 62 (f), Peter Zurek 36bl; **Thinkstock:** Comstock 76l, and iStockphoto 48 (c), 48 (e).

All other images © Pearson Education Limited

**Screenshots:** Screenshot on page 76 front cover of Diary of a Wimpy Kid by Jeff Kinney (First published in the US by Harry N. Abrams 2007, Puffin Books 2008). Copyright © Jeff Kinney, 2007. Reproduced by permission of Penguin Books Ltd.

Every effort has been made to trace the copyright holders and we apologize in advance for any unintentional omissions. We would be pleased to insert the appropriate acknowledgement in any subsequent edition of this publication.

# Contents

# Scope and sequence

## Welcome

| | |
|---|---|
| Vocabulary | **Senses:** look, smell, taste, sound, feel |
| Structures | Does it look good? Yes, it does. / No, it doesn't.<br>What does it look like? It looks good.<br>It looks like a cake. |

## 1 Adventure camp

| | |
|---|---|
| Vocabulary | **Camping equipment:** sleeping bag, tent, poles, pegs, compass, flashlight<br>**Camping activities:** pitch the tent, take down the tent, put in the pegs, lay out the bed, cover our heads, light a fire, keep out the rain, read a compass |
| Structures | Flo is good at swimming.<br>I like hiking, but I don't like sailing.<br>I love fishing and camping.<br>I'm pitching the tent.<br>We're putting in the pegs.<br>I can pitch a tent, but I can't read a compass. |

**Cross-curricular:**
**Social science:**
Being a mountaineer and an adventurer

**Values:** Safety first. Think about safety when you go camping.

## 2 Wildlife park

| | |
|---|---|
| Vocabulary | **Animals:** rhino, cheetah, panther, lemur, koala, whale, seal, otter, sea turtle, tiger<br>**Superlative adjectives:** tallest, longest, shortest, biggest, smallest, heaviest, lightest, fastest, slowest |
| Structures | How heavy is it? It's 800 kilograms.<br>How tall is it? It's five meters tall.<br>The giraffe is taller than the rhino.<br>The giraffe is the tallest.<br>Are otters bigger than seals? Yes, they are. / No, they aren't.<br>Were the giraffes taller than the trees? Yes, they were. / No, they weren't.<br>Which is the heaviest? The hippo is the heaviest. |

**Cross-curricular:**
**Science:** Chameleons

**Values:** Think before you act. Think carefully before making important decisions.

## 3 Where we live

| | |
|---|---|
| Vocabulary | **Places:** supermarket, library, park, movie theater, shopping mall, museum, hospital, airport, bookstore, station, arcade, video store |
| Structures | How do you get to the supermarket? Turn left at the corner, then go straight.<br>The supermarket is behind the school.<br>I want to go to the park.<br>He/She wants to go to the park.<br>I have to go to the library.<br>He/She has to go to the library. |

**Cross-curricular:**
**Geography:**
Interesting places

**Values:** Learn to be flexible. It's often frustrating to do what you don't want to do.

## 4 Good days and bad days

| | |
|---|---|
| Vocabulary | **International food dishes:** curry, an omelet, spaghetti, fish and chips, paella, dumplings, sushi, stew, rice and beans<br>**Verbs and objects:** pack my bag, miss the bus, pass a test, eat my lunch, bring my juice, drop the ball |
| Structures | I cooked stew.<br>He dropped the plate.<br>She paddled very quickly.<br>We fell in the lake.<br>What happened? I didn't pass my test because I didn't study.<br>He didn't bring his juice because he was late for school. |

**Cross-curricular:**
**Social science:**
Ellen the sailor

**Values:** Be positive about your day. Don't worry. Be happy.

##  5 Trips

| Vocabulary | **Tourist attractions:** aquarium, amusement park, palace, water park, theater, national park, circus |
| --- | --- |
| | **Amusement park attractions:** ride the Ferris wheel, go on the bumper cars, play miniature golf, ride the carousel, go on the paddle boats, ride the roller coaster, go on the pirate ship, go on the water slide |
| Structures | What did you do yesterday? I went to the aquarium. |
| | Did you go to the aquarium? Yes, I did. / No, I didn't. |
| | Did you like the aquarium? Yes, I did. / No, I didn't. |
| | What will you do at the amusement park? |
| | First, I'll ride the Ferris wheel. Then, I'll go on the bumper cars. |

**Cross-curricular:**
**Social science:** Beach safety

**Values:** Plan, but be flexible. Planning helps you do more things.

##  6 Arts and entertainment

| Vocabulary | **Movie genres:** thriller, comedy, sci-fi, romance, musical, cartoon |
| --- | --- |
| | **Musical instruments:** cello, harmonica, saxophone, triangle, drums, clarinet, harp, tambourine |
| Structures | I saw the movie by myself. |
| | You wrote it by yourself. |
| | He made it by himself. |
| | She didn't go to the movie by herself. |
| | We didn't watch it by ourselves. |
| | They didn't draw it by themselves. |
| | Did you hear the cello? Yes, I did. / No, I didn't. |
| | Have you ever played the saxophone? Yes, I have. / No, I haven't. |
| | Have you ever been to a concert? Yes, I have. / No, I've never been to a concert. |

**Cross-curricular:**
**Literature:** Poetry

**Values:** Learn to be self-sufficient. You can always do some things by yourself.

##  7 Space

| Vocabulary | **Space:** an astronaut, a planet, a comet, a telescope, an alien, a spaceship, the moon, a satellite, a star |
| --- | --- |
| | **Adjectives:** complicated, amazing, frightening, intelligent, brilliant, important |
| Structures | Who are they? They're astronauts. |
| | When did they come? They came last night. |
| | Where did they come from? They came from the moon. |
| | How did they get here? They came by spaceship. |
| | Why are you looking at the sky? I saw a flashing light. |
| | What's that flashing light? It's a spaceship. |
| | Which telescope is more complicated? The big telescope is more complicated than the small telescope. |
| | Which telescope is the most complicated? The big telescope is the most complicated. |
| | Which telescope is less complicated? The small telescope is less complicated than the big telescope. |
| | Which telescope is the least complicated? The small telescope is the least complicated. |

**Cross-curricular:**
**Science:** Space facts

**Values:** Use your imagination when you are trying to solve a problem.

## 8 The environment

| Vocabulary | **Ways to help the environment:** recycle paper, recycle bottles, collect garbage, reuse plastic bags, turn off the lights, use public transportation |
| --- | --- |
| | **Environmentally friendly outcomes:** recycle paper / save trees, recycle bottles / save resources, collect garbage / keep the planet clean, reuse plastic bags / reduce waste, turn off the lights / conserve energy, use public transportation / reduce pollution |
| Structures | Are you going to recycle paper? Yes, I am. / No, I'm not. I'm going to recycle bottles. |
| | What can you do to help? I can use public transportation. |
| | If you reuse plastic bags, you'll reduce waste. |

**Cross-curricular:**
**Geography:** Our amazing world

**Values:** Save our planet. Learn to save energy and keep the planet clean.

# Welcome

1. I like the new sign, Dad. It looks great. Hi, Chris!

2. Woof!!! Snarl!!!

   What's that noise?

   Quick! Let's look!

   Sounds dangerous. Be careful!

3. Wild dogs!

   Scat! Go away!

4. There's something in the tree! Look!

   Oh! It's a chimpanzee! He looks swee

5. We can look after him in the nature reserve.

6. I can look after him, Dad.

   Hello, chimp! Your name is Champ, and you have a new mom!

6

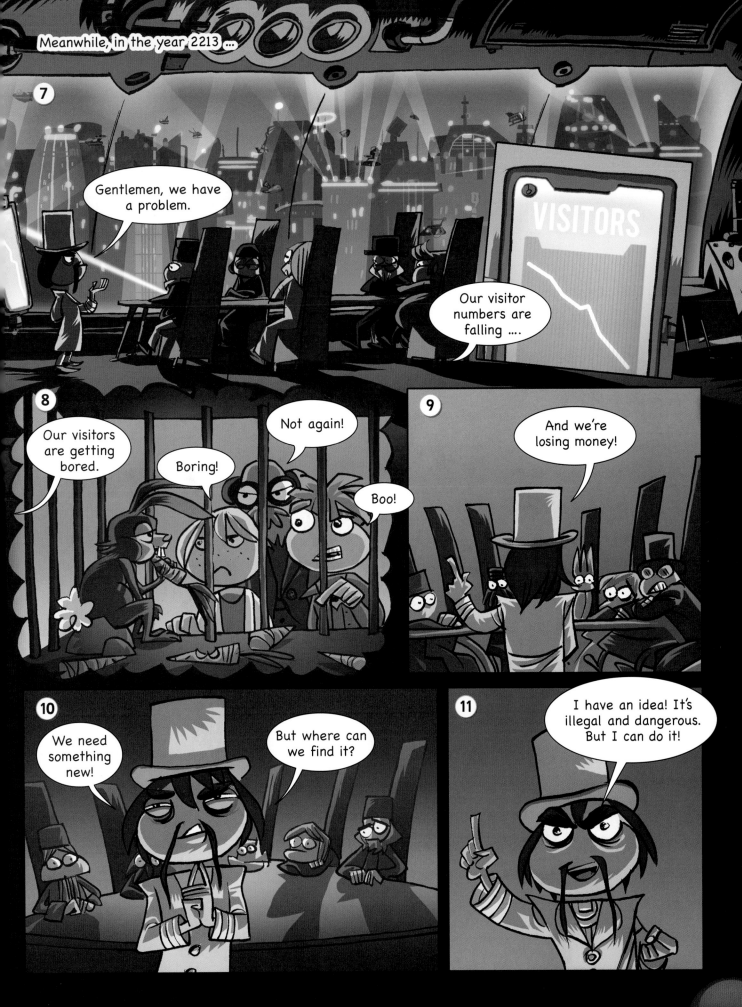

# Year 2213

**1** This is Serena. Serena is outside all the time and knows a lot. She's good at running and jumping. She can climb walls, too!

Serena

**2** Zero Zendell

# Present day

**1** This is Marta, who lives with her parents in a nature reserve. She's brave but sometimes gets into arguments quickly. She goes everywhere with her chimpanzee, Champ.

Marta

**2** This is Chris. Chris has long, dark hair. He's a smart boy but he's not so active—not like Marta. But they are good friends. He likes to think carefully about things, too. Chris doesn't like getting wet or dirty.

Chris

**3**

Champ

*Character introductions*

**2** Work with a friend and write. What things can you see on Future Island that we do not have now?

1 _____

2 _____

3 _____

4 _____

5 _____

**3** (A:03) Listen and read about Serena and Zero Zendell. Then write.

**a** What does Zero Zendell do on Future Island?

He _____.

**b** What is Zero Zendell's problem?

His zoo _____.

**c** What is Serena good at?

She is good at _____ and _____.

**d** What unusual thing can Serena do?

She can _____.

This is Zero Zendell. He always wears a top hat and has a long mustache. He has the only animals on Future Island in his zoo. But the people are bored with seeing the same animals. Zero Zendell has a plan to make his zoo more popular, but it's illegal and dangerous!

**4** (A:04) Listen and read about Marta, Chris, and Champ. Then circle T = True or F = False.

| | |
|---|---|
| **a** Marta is brave. | T / F |
| **b** Marta's unusual pet is a chimpanzee. | T / F |
| **c** Chris rescued Champ. | T / F |
| **d** Champ lives in the nature reserve now. | T / F |
| **e** Chris is an active boy. | T / F |
| **f** Chris is Marta's brother. | T / F |

**5** Ask and answer.

1 Who do you think are the bad guys in this story?

2 What do you think Zero Zendell's plan is to make the zoo more popular?

This is Champ, the chimpanzee. Wild dogs were trying to attack him so Marta's dad rescued him. Now Marta looks after Champ. Champ is always very friendly and he's happy with his new life in the nature reserve.

**6** A:06 **Listen and say.**

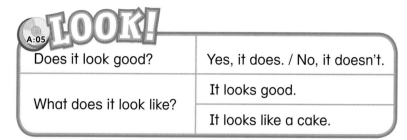

A:05 **LOOK!**

| Does it look good? | Yes, it does. / No, it doesn't. |
| What does it look like? | It looks good. |
| | It looks like a cake. |

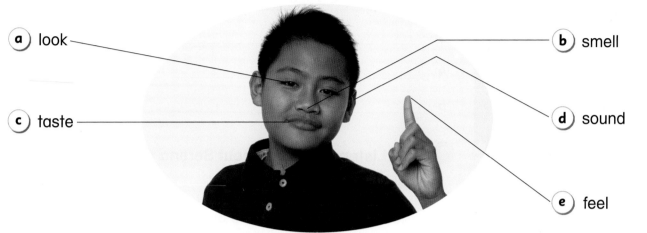

**a** look

**b** smell

**c** taste

**d** sound

**e** feel

**7** A:07 **Listen and check (✓). Then number.**

| | | looks | | | feels | | | smells / sounds / tastes | | |
|---|---|---|---|---|---|---|---|---|---|---|
| 1 | scary ☐ | hard ☐ | | spiky ☐ | soft ☐ | | nice ☐ | sweet ☐ |
| 2 | round ☐ | red ☐ | | smooth ☐ | hard ☐ | | loud ☐ | quiet ☐ |
| 3 | cute ☐ | scary ☐ | | hot ☐ | furry ☐ | | | |
| 4 | wild ☐ | wet ☐ | | cold ☐ | hot ☐ | | | |

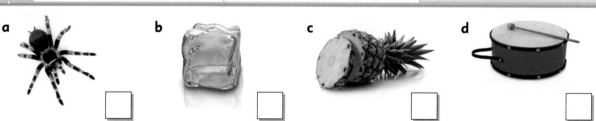

**a** ☐   **b** ☐   **c** ☐   **d** ☐

**8** **Look at Activity 7 and write.**

1  The _____ feels _____ and tastes _____ .

2  The _____ looks _____ and _____ loud.

3  The _____ .

4  The ice cube _____ .

**9** **Ask and answer.**

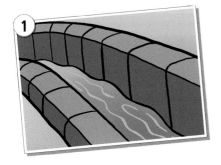

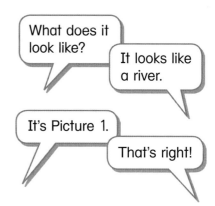

What does it look like?

It looks like a river.

It's Picture 1.

That's right!

 **10** **Play the guessing game.**

 **How to play**

Your friend looks at Number 1 and thinks of a fruit. Ask questions. "Does it taste sweet?" "Does it feel spiky?" Check (✓) the question box each time you ask a question. How many questions did it take to get the correct fruit? Play again with Number 2.

Check (✓) a box each time you ask a question. How many questions did you ask?

|  | Question 1 | Question 2 | Question 3 | Question 4 | Question 5 | Question 6 | Question 7 | Question 8 |
|---|---|---|---|---|---|---|---|---|
| **1** fruit |  |  |  |  |  |  |  |  |
| **2** vegetable |  |  |  |  |  |  |  |  |
| **3** clothes |  |  |  |  |  |  |  |  |
| **4** drink |  |  |  |  |  |  |  |  |
| **5** animal |  |  |  |  |  |  |  |  |

# Adventure camp

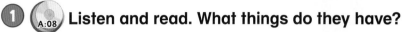

**1** **A:08** **Listen and read. What things do they have?**

**1**
Hi, I'm Hannah. Welcome to this summer's adventure camp.

**2**
OK. I can see your sleeping bags, but who has the tent, poles, and pegs?

I have the tent, Felipe has the poles, and Maria has the pegs.

I have a big flashlight and four compasses.

**3**
OK. Let's pitch the tent and make a campfire.

Great!

**4**
This is the week's schedule. There's lots to do!

**2** **A:09** **Listen and say.**

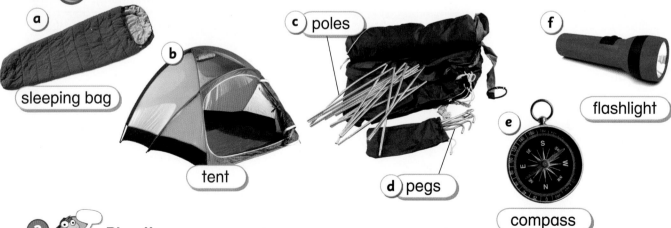

**a** sleeping bag

**b** tent

**c** poles

**d** pegs

**e** compass

**f** flashlight

**3** **Play the memory game.**

**A:** I went camping and in my tent there was a sleeping bag.

**B:** I went camping and in my tent there was a sleeping bag and a ....

*Camping equipment*

**4**   **Read. Then circle T = True or F = False.**

**a**

My name's Tom. I'm fourteen and I'm American. I love playing basketball and soccer. I can cook and swim, but I can't surf. I have one sister, Flo. She's twelve and she's very funny.

**b**

My name's Maria and I'm thirteen. I'm from Mexico. I like dancing, but I'm not very good at singing! I have two sisters. They're eight and ten and I love playing with them!

**c**

I'm Flo and I'm twelve. I'm from the United States. I'm good at swimming. I love talking to my friends. I have one brother. He's fourteen and he's very good at sports. He's very clever, too.

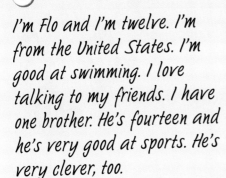

**d**

I'm Felipe. I'm from Spain. I'm thirteen. I love playing video games and I like science and math. I have three brothers and they love video games, too. We always have competitions!

1 Tom can swim and surf.          T / F

2 Flo is good at swimming.         T / F

3 Flo loves talking to her friends.   T / F

4 Maria is Mexican.                T / F

5 Felipe has only two brothers.     T / F

**LOOK!**

Flo is good at swimming.

I like hiking, but I don't like sailing.

I love fishing and camping.

**5**  **Ask and answer.**

1 Where are Tom and Flo from?
2 What does Tom love doing?
3 How old are Maria's sisters?
4 What subjects does Felipe like?

**6**  **Imagine you are Tom, Maria, Flo, or Felipe. Ask and answer.**

1 How old are you?
2 Where are you from?
3 What do you like doing?
4 What are you good at?
5 Do you have any brothers or sisters?

**7** (A:12) **Listen and say.**

**a** pitch the tent

**b** take down the tent

**c** put in the pegs

**d** lay out the bed

**e** cover our heads

**f** light a fire

**g** keep out the rain

**h** read a compass

**8** (A:13-14) **Listen to the song and write.**

Scouts from all around the world, from Spain to Mexico.
We're traveling together, from the mountains to the sea.
We're walking for miles and learning every day.

We're reading a _____ and finding our way.

**Chorus:**

*Oh, we are adventure campers, here is our song.*
*With adventure and new friends, you can't go wrong!*

At the end of the day we're back to camp again.

We're pitching our _____, they keep out the rain.

We're putting in the _____ and laying out our _____.

We're sleeping in _____ that cover our heads!

(Chorus)

All this adventure is making us fit and strong.
We're cooking our food, which doesn't take too long.
We're eating our dinner, and then we're so tired.

We're sleeping in tents all around the _____!

(Chorus)

**9** **Look at Activity 8 and check (✓) the activities in the song.**

| | | |
|---|---|---|
| 1 reading a compass ☐ | | 2 wearing sunglasses ☐ |
| 3 pitching tents ☐ | | 4 putting in the pegs ☐ |
| 5 running a race ☐ | | 6 taking down the tent ☐ |

**10** Listen and stick. Then write and say.

**LOOK!**

A:15

I'm pitching the tent.

We're putting in the pegs.

I can pitch a tent, but I can't read a compass.

**1**

He's _____

_____.

**2**

She's _____

_____.

**3**

He's _____

_____.

Stick

**4**

She's _____

_____.

**5**

He's _____

_____.

**6**

They're _____

_____.

**7**

They're _____

_____.

He's pitching the tent.

 **11** Imagine what they can/can't do and match. Then say.

can                                            can't

**1**

**a**           **b**

**2**

**c**          **d**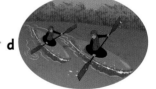

**3**

**e**           **f**

**4**

**g**           **h**

Felipe can cook fish, but he can't kayak.

**12**   **Read. Where was Flo yesterday?**

*Dear Mom,*

*How are you? It's our second day at adventure camp and we're having a great time. We have some new friends, too—they're from Spain and Mexico. They're teaching me Spanish, but I'm not very good at it!*

*Our first night was great. There was a big dinner to welcome everyone and there were songs by the campfire. After the campfire we went to bed. At night our tent was cold, but it was warm in the sleeping bag.*

*Today, we're walking to a wildlife park that's next to the camp.*

*Here's a photo of me with my new friends and a photo of last night's campfire.*

*Love to you and Dad,*

*Flo*

**13** **Read and circle. Then write the correct sentence.**

1  Flo's new friends are from Spain and ( Italy / Mexico ).

_____

2  Flo is learning ( Italian / Spanish ).

_____

3  There was a big ( lunch / dinner ) on their first day.

_____

4  It ( was / wasn't ) cold in the sleeping bag.

_____

5  Today, they're ( walking / running ) to a wildlife park.

_____

**14**  **Ask and answer.**

1  Do you like camping?
2  Where do you go camping?
3  What activities do you do there?

**15**  **Read. What is Bear's job?**

**Bear Grylls**

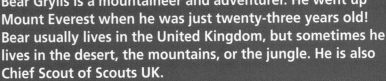

Bear Grylls is a mountaineer and adventurer. He went up Mount Everest when he was just twenty-three years old! Bear usually lives in the United Kingdom, but sometimes he lives in the desert, the mountains, or the jungle. He is also Chief Scout of Scouts UK.

**1 What do you like doing?**
I like playing the guitar, running, doing yoga, and playing with my children.

**2 Do you like living in the jungle?**
I love jungles but they're difficult to live in. There are often a lot of snakes and insects. Sometimes I sleep up a tree and when it rains, it's horrible.

**3 Where is your favorite place?**
An island in Indonesia. I love visiting islands and this one was really beautiful.

**4 What do you do before an adventure?**
I always learn a lot about where I want to go—I learn about the plants and animals. I train six days a week and I run and do yoga, too.

**5 Are you scared of anything?**
Yes, I'm scared of high buildings and mountains. I can go to the top of high buildings but I don't like it.

**16**  **Circle T = True or F = False.**

**1** Bear likes running and doing yoga.              T / F

**2** There are often snakes and insects in the jungle.    T / F

**3** Bear's favorite place is in the United Kingdom.    T / F

**4** Bear doesn't like high buildings and mountains.    T / F

**THINK!**

Look at these lists. What doesn't belong?

For the jungle: insect repellent, sunblock, scarf

For the sea: sunblock, snow boots, fresh water

For camping: flashlight, in-line skates, matches

**17** **Look at Activity 15. Ask and answer questions 1, 3, and 5 with a friend.**

 Imagine you're going to the jungle. Write a list of ten things you should take and why.

**18**  A:19 **Listen and read.**

STORY

**1** MONKEY ROCK Nature Reserve

Hi, Marta. Hi, Champ.

Bye, Mom! We're going to the amusement park.

Ook!

**2** ZERO ZENDELL'S TIME MACHINE

Hello my dears! I like your pet!

**3** Come and try my time machine! Only one dollar.

I love traveling.

Er ... Marta! I like traveling, too. But I don't like talking to this man.

**4** Wow. This is cool. We can go to the future!

FLASH

**5** Wow! Look! It's strange. I know this place ....

It's fantastic! Look at the cars!

**6** FLASH

What was that?

The time machine! It isn't here! And where's Champ?

**19**  **Why does Chris say he knows the place? Discuss your answers.**

**20**  **Circle T = True or F = False.**

1 Marta and Chris travel to the future.       T / F

2 Zero Zendell doesn't like pet chimpanzees.       T / F

3 Zero Zendell has a time machine.       T / F

4 Chris likes talking to Zero Zendell.       T / F

5 Zero Zendell is taller than the children.       T / F

6 Marta's dad takes Champ.       T / F

**21** **Role-play the story.**

**22**  **Number to match the instructions to the headings.**

**VALUES**

Safety first. Think about safety when you go camping.

☐ Food and water       ☐ Making a fire       ☐ Things you need

☐ Pitching the tent       ☐ Choosing the right spot

**1**

Always choose a flat, high spot to set up camp—not near a river or mountain slope.

**2**

Clean the ground and pitch the tent. The door should face the rising sun.

**3**

The fire shouldn't be too close to the tents or under tree branches.

**4**
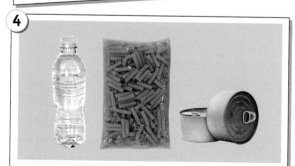
Take a lot of drinking water, dry foods (pasta, noodles, rice, cookies, nuts, and raisins), and canned foods (soups and vegetables).

**5**

Take insect repellent, sunblock, a first aid kit, a flashlight, matches, batteries, and a gas stove.

**HOME-SCHOOL LINK**

Tell your family why camping safety is important.

**PARENT**

**23** **Play the game.**

**HAVE FUN!**

- ● I'm good at ....
- ● I love ....
- ○ I like ..., but I don't like....
- ● I can ..., but I can't ....

I'm good at swimming.

**START**

**1**

**2** You didn't bring the pegs. Throw a 3 to continue.

**3**

**4** It's sunny. Move 1 space.

**5**

**6** You're good at pitching the tent. Move 2 spaces.

**19**

**FINISH**

**7**

**8**

**18** You didn't bring a sleeping bag. Throw a 6 to continue.

**9** It starts raining before you finish pitching the tent. Miss a turn.

**17**

**16**

**10**

**15** You find new wood for the fire and cook dinner. Move 2 spaces.

**14**

**13** You get wood for the fire but it's wet! Miss a turn.

**11** It's dark but you have a flashlight and new batteries. Take another turn.

**12**

**24** (A:20) **Listen and write ✓ or ✗.**

| | | likes | | loves | | is good at |
|---|---|---|---|---|---|---|
| 1 Sally | a | ☐ | b | ☐ | c | ☐ |
| 2 Pete | a | ☐ | b | ☐ | c | ☐ |
| 3 Brad | a | ☐ | b | ☐ | c | ☐ |
| 4 Jo | a | ☐ | b | ☐ | c | ☐ |

**25**   **Unscramble and write questions. Then look at Activity 24 and write the answers.**

1 Sally / doing / love / does / what

_____    _____

2 Pete / a / is / compass / at / reading / good

_____    _____

3 Brad / what / doing / like / doesn't

_____    _____

4 Jo / what / at / good / is

_____    _____

 I can say what I'm good at and what I like/don't like doing. ☐

I can say what I'm doing now. ☐

  TEACHER

Now go to Future Island.

a

**1** Look at photos a–c and make sentences.

> There's a cave.
> There are some trees.

**2** A:21 Listen and read. Then number.

1

2

Camping in Thailand is a lot of fun. My favorite place is a National Park called Khao Sam Roi Yot. Khao Sam Roi Yot means the mountain with 300 peaks. The mountains are very difficult to climb. There are a lot of things to see around the park. I like watching the lovely birds and other wild animals like deer and squirrels. There are a lot of interesting caves, too. Thailand is an exciting place!

**Alak, 12, Thailand**

Death Valley National Park in California is a great place for desert camping. It's very hot there in the summer. I usually visit Death Valley in the spring with my family. I love riding my bike on the paths in the mountains. Mountain biking is difficult but it's very exciting. My dad likes making big campfires in the evening. He likes cooking our dinner on the fire. There are many types of snakes, lizards, and birds in Death Valley. It's never boring in the desert!

**Melissa, 12, United States**

**b**

**c**

**3**

Vulcano is a small volcanic island in Italy. I like camping there in the summer with my grandparents. We sleep in a small cabin in the forest. During the day, my grandpa rides a motorbike around the island. I like hiking to the top of the volcano. My grandma likes walking on the black sandy beaches near the sea. There is special mud in Vulcano that is very good for your skin. Some people like putting the mud on their bodies. I love visiting Vulcano!

Luca, 11, Italy

**3**  **Circle T = True or F = False.**

1  The mountains of Thailand are easy to climb.                    T / F
2  Alak likes watching birds.                                       T / F
3  Death Valley is in the desert.                                   T / F
4  Melissa doesn't like riding her bike.   T / F
5  Vulcano is a big island.                                         T / F
6  Luca likes hiking.                                               T / F

**4** **Ask and answer.**

1  Do you like camping?
2  Where can you camp in your country?

**YOUR TURN!**

**Describe an ideal camping trip. Think about these things.**

What's the place's name? Where is it?
What's the place like?
What can you do there?
What should you take with you?
Why is it ideal for you?

# 2 Wildlife park

**1** **A:22** **Listen and read. Where was Flo?**

**1**

**2**
- We were with the cheetahs. They were really fast!
- Cheetahs are the fastest animals on earth.

What did you learn today?

**3**
I was with the snakes. They were really long. One of them is the longest type of snake in the world!

**4**
- I was with the elephant.
- Cool! How big was it?
- Really big, and heavy— it's 3,000 kilograms! And it was really naughty!

**2** **A:23** **Listen and say.**

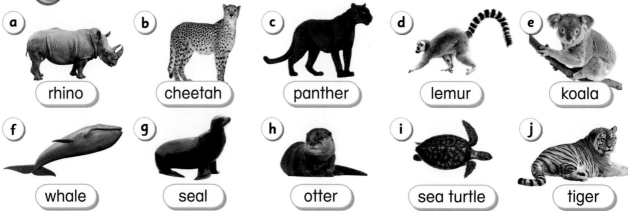

| a | b | c | d | e |
|---|---|---|---|---|
| rhino | cheetah | panther | lemur | koala |

| f | g | h | i | j |
|---|---|---|---|---|
| whale | seal | otter | sea turtle | tiger |

**3** **Play the game. How many animals can you guess?**

**A:** Long and thin!    **B:** Snakes!

**4**   **Look and listen. Tom is with which animal?**

Name:        Roddy
How heavy?   1,600 kilograms
How tall?    two meters
How long?    three meters
How fast?    fast!

Name:        Geri
How heavy?   800 kilograms
How tall?    five meters
How long?    three meters
How fast?    fast!

**5**  **Look at Activity 4 and make questions. Then ask and answer.**

1  tall / the giraffe?
2  heavy / the rhino?
3  fast / the rhino?
4  long / the giraffe?
5  tall / the rhino?
6  heavy / the giraffe?

A:25 **LOOK!**

| How heavy is it? | It's 800 kilograms. |
| How tall is it? | It's five meters tall. |
| The giraffe is taller than the rhino. | |
| The giraffe is the tallest. | |

How tall is the giraffe?

It's five meters tall.

**6**  **Ask and answer to guess the animal.**

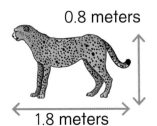

0.8 meters

1.8 meters

1.2 meters

2.5 meters

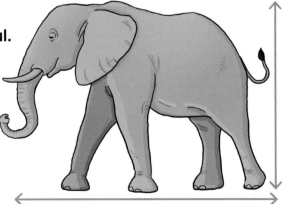

3.5 meters

7 meters

A:  How tall is it?
B:  It's 3.5 meters tall.

**7** A:26 **Listen and say.**

a tallest

b longest

c shortest

d biggest

e smallest

f heaviest

g lightest

h fastest

i slowest

**8** A:27-28 **Listen to the song and write.**

**Chorus:**

Take me to a place where the days are _____,
Where I can be with the animals, wild and free.
Take me to a place where the trees are _____,
Than the houses and the buildings in the big city.

In the sea there are seals, _____ than otters.
There are blue whales, _____ than my street.
Can you see the turtles, swimming in the blue water?
They're _____ than my pet fish, but they have feet.

**(Chorus)**

In the jungle there are tigers, _____ taxis.
There are panthers, _____ the night.
I want to see the lemurs, sitting in the trees.
I really love wild animals, orange, black, or white.
Orange, black, or white.
Orange, black, or white.

**9** **Look at Activity 8. How many animals are in the song?**

# LOOK!

| | |
|---|---|
| Are otters bigger than seals? | Yes, they are.<br>No, they aren't. |
| Were the giraffes taller than the trees? | Yes, they were.<br>No, they weren't. |
| Which is the heaviest? | The hippo is the heaviest. |

**10** (A:30) **Listen and write. Then ask and answer.**

1 heavy   _____   _____   _____   light

2 fast    _____   _____   _____   slow

3 loud    _____   _____   _____   quiet

4 long    _____   _____   _____   short

Which is the heaviest?   The whale is the heaviest.

**11**  **Write.**

1 giraffes / otters / tigers

(tall): Giraffes are the tallest. Tigers are taller than otters. _____

2 koalas / lemurs / turtles

(slow): _____

3 elephants / turtles / hippos

(heavy): _____

4 panthers / giraffes / cheetahs

(fast): _____

**12** **Ask questions. Guess the animal.**

A: Is it heavier than a hippo?   B: No, it isn't.
A: Is it faster than a panther?  B: Yes, it is.
A: It's a cheetah!               B: That's right!

**13**   **Read. Is Vernie happier now?**

## PLEASE SPONSOR VERNIE!

### Vernie's story

Here at the reserve, we have a lot of rescued koalas. They live longer here, and they are happier here than in the wild.

Vernie the koala was in the wild for years. Her home was next to a road. It was very dangerous. Her joey, a baby koala, died one day on the road. Vernie was very sad.

We went to the forest one day, looking for sick koalas. Vernie was next to the road. She was not happy and she was sick.

Now, she is safe, happy, and healthy in our koala reserve. Please sponsor her!

Please sponsor me!

To sponsor Vernie now, click on this link.

**14**  **Write.**

1 Where was Vernie's home? _____

2 What does "joey" mean? _____

3 Was Vernie happier in the wild? _____

4 Was Vernie healthy in the wild? _____

5 Where is Vernie now? _____

**15**  **Write. Think of two animals from each place.**

| 1 | Australia | |
|---|---|---|
| 2 | Asia | |
| 3 | Africa | |

**16** (A:32) **Read. Can you find the chameleons in the pictures?**

**SCIENCE 2**

SEARCH

# Cool camouflage for chameleons!

**Interesting fact:** Chameleon means "small lion" but they are cousins of the lizard.

**Size:** They are sometimes smaller than your finger. Some are longer than your arm! Females are often smaller than males.

**Body:** They have very long tongues and their feet have claws. They are very good at climbing.

**Color:** Chameleons are very clever—they use color to show how they feel or to hide. They can change color when they are nervous, scared, hot, or cold. A panther chameleon turns red when it is angry.

**Places:** A lot of chameleons live in Madagascar in Africa. Some live in India, too. They like hot, dry places.

**Food:** Chameleons eat insects and they are good at catching flies with their long tongues. Meller's chameleons are big chameleons and they also eat small birds.

**17** **Ask and answer.**

1 What do chameleons look like?
2 When do they change color?
3 Where do they live?
4 What do they eat?
5 What are the names of some types of chameleons?

## THINK!

Chameleons use camouflage to protect themselves from predators. What do you think these animals use for protection?

**skunks turtles gazelles**

MINI- **PROJECT** Find out about a strange and interesting animal. Then write about it.

**18** A:33 **Listen and read.**

**STORY**

**1**

You're funny! Where are you from?

We're not funny! You're funnier than us!

We're lost. And we can't find our chimpanzee.

**2**

Chimpanzee?! Wow! Are you rich?

No, we aren't. We were in this time machine and it disappeared ....

**3**

Hmm. They say Zero Zendell has a time machine. And he wants animals at any price.

Do you think Champ is valuable?

Of course!

**4**

This park is very small.

Park? It's a museum! And you can't sit on the grass! The guards ....

**5**

Hey!

Run! They're coming!

I'm OK. I'm faster than they are.

**6**

Phew! That was close! Thanks.

We're lost. We can't go home. And we can't find Champ.

Don't worry, I'm your friend and I want to help you.

**19**  **Why does Serena think Marta and Chris are rich? Discuss your answers.**

**20** **Circle T = True or F = False.**

1 Marta and Chris are rich.      T / F

2 Champ is valuable.      T / F

3 Chris sits on the grass because he thinks it is a museum.      T / F

4 The museum guards run after them.      T / F

5 Marta and Chris are lost and they can't find Champ.      T / F

6 Marta and Chris have a new friend.      T / F

**21** **Role-play the story.**

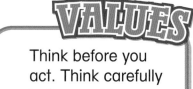

**VALUES**

Think before you act. Think carefully before making important decisions.

**22**  **Read the situations. Check (✓) the best thing to do.**

| | 1 | 2 | 3 |
|---|---|---|---|
| **A** Tomorrow is the deadline for entering a story writing competition. What do you do? | You're not happy with your writing, but you sign up immediately. | You're not happy with your writing. You ask your teacher for advice and then decide. | You don't enter the competition because you're not happy with your writing. |
| **B** Your best friend is not talking to you. He/She looks angry but you don't know why. What do you do? | You text your friend and invite him/her to meet you after school. | You leave a note on your friend's desk to ask what's wrong. | You find your friend at school and ask what's wrong. |
| **C** You want to try out for the school band but you aren't very good. What do you do? | You try out anyway. | You ask a friend or teacher to help you practice. | You don't try out at all. |

**HOME-SCHOOL LINK**

Tell your family about an important decision you made today.

**PARENT**

23  Read the clues. Write the animals' names.

**Down** ↓

1  It's the second largest of all land animals and has one or two horns.

2  It looks like a small monkey and has a long tail.

4  It's the largest land animal.

5  It's an orange cat with black stripes.

9  It's an African animal that has black and white stripes.

10  It's a large animal with flippers. It eats fish and lives in and near the sea.

13  This animal is the "king" of the animal world.

**Across** →

3  It's the fastest land animal in the world.

6  It's a very large mammal that lives in the sea.

7  This animal eats fish and is about 1 meter long.

8  It's in the cat family and is usually black.

11  It's a large sea reptile that has a thick shell.

12  It's quieter than a chimpanzee but much bigger.

14  It's an Australian animal that looks like a small bear.

**24** Listen, check (✓), and circle.

**1**

longer / shorter

**2**

bigger / faster

**3**

lighter / taller

**4**

fastest / faster

**5**

fastest / heaviest

**6**

lightest / biggest

**25**  Look at Activity 24 and write.

1 The lemur's tail is longer than the rhino's tail.

2 _____

3 _____

4 _____

5 _____

6 _____

 I can use measurements to describe animals. ☐

I can compare animals. ☐

 TEACHER

 Now go to Future Island.

# Review Units 1 and 2

**1** Unscramble and write the camping words.

1 plesengi gba
2 slope
3 etnt
4 spge
5 ihtglfhsal
6 mosacsp

_____  _____  _____  _____  _____  _____

**2**  Read and number.

1 I'm putting in the pegs.
2 He's laying out the bed.
3 The tent is keeping out the rain.
4 She's covering her head.
5 We're pitching a tent.

**a**  **b**  **c**  **d**  **e**

**3** A:35 Read and circle.

> Hello, I'm Hannah. I'm studying to be a vet. I don't like working in offices, but I love working with animals. I like camping, too. I'm good at climbing and pitching tents. I'm working as a youth leader at adventure camp. Last summer I went to Brazil. I was a youth leader at Camp Paulo. It was very hot in Brazil, but there were a lot of interesting animals.

1 Hannah is studying to be a ….

  **a** cook       **b** vet       **c** youth leader

2 She's good at ….

  **a** climbing    **b** trampolining    **c** diving

3 Last summer Hannah went to ….

  **a** Argentina    **b** England    **c** Brazil

4 It was very … at Camp Paulo.

  **a** cold    **b** hot    **c** rainy

5 There were a lot of interesting … there.

  **a** insects    **b** flowers    **c** animals

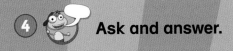 **Ask and answer.**

**Picture A**

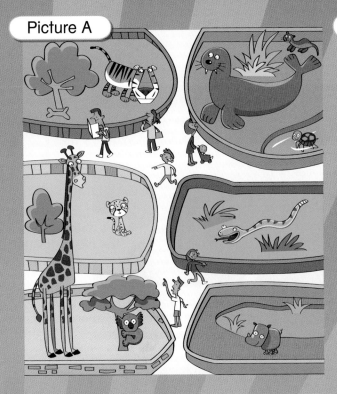

**Picture B**

**A:** The giraffe is taller than the rhino.
**B:** It's Picture A.

**A:** The snake is the longest.
**B:** It's Picture B.

**A:** Which koala is the biggest?
**B:** The koala in Picture A is the biggest.

**A:** Which animal is the heaviest?
**B:** I think the seal in Picture A is the heaviest.

*Guess!*

5  **Guess the animal. Write.**

1 It likes eating leaves. It's the tallest animal in the world. _____

2 It likes swimming in rivers. It eats meat. It has a long tail and
 big teeth. _____

3 It has five fingers but it doesn't have a tail. It can climb trees. _____

4 It's big and heavy. It has a big mouth and a horn. _____

5 It likes eating meat. It has a long tail. It's the fastest land animal
 in the world. _____

6 It can't run, but it can climb trees. _____

*Guess!*

# 3 Where we live

**1** *(A:36)* **Listen and read. What is Flo doing?**

Phew! 450 steps!

I'm hot now! I want to go swimming! Where's the swimming pool?

It's there—near the movie theater.

Then we can go to the park, there, opposite the school. But where's Flo?

Look! She's there—near the park. What's she doing?

She's buying ice cream! I want ice cream, too! Come on!

**2** *(A:37)* **Listen and say.**

a  supermarket

b  library

c  park

d  movie theater

e  shopping mall

f  museum

**3** **Look at Activity 1. What places can you see?**

**Listen and check (✓). Then say.**

1 **a**  **b**

2 **a**  **b**

3 **a**  **b**

The van is in front of the supermarket.

**A:39** **LOOK!**

How do you get to the supermarket?

Turn left at the corner, then go straight.

The supermarket is behind the school.

5  **Stick. Then work with a friend. Give directions to each place.**

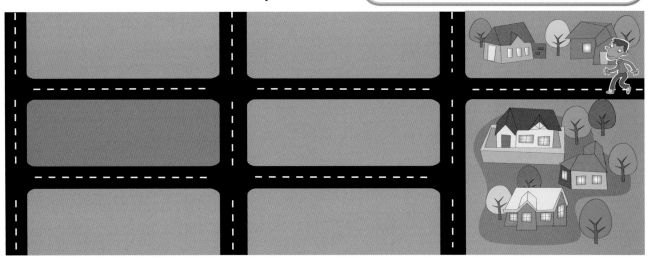

**A:** How do you get to the swimming pool?

**B:** Go straight. Turn left at the next corner, then go straight. Turn right at the movie theater. It's next to the movie theater and opposite the park.

**6**  **Listen and say.**

**a**
hospital

**b**
airport

**c**
bookstore

**d**
station

**e**
arcade

**f**
video store

**7**  **Listen to the song and write.**

SONG

I want to go to the _____.
Do you want to come with me?
Sorry, I can't, my friend.
I want to go to the shopping mall,
But I have to do other things.

Chorus:
*There are many things I want to do.*
*But I can't, my friend. I can't today.*
I have to go to the _____.
I have to go to the _____.
I have to go to the _____,
*to pick up a friend.*

I want to go to the _____.
Do you want to come with me?
Sorry, I can't, my friend.
I want to go to the movie theater,
But I have to do other things.

(Chorus)

I want to go to _____.
Do you want to come with me?
Sorry, I can't, my friend.
I want to go to the park,
But I have to do other things.

(Chorus)

**8**  **Listen again and write.**

Where does the girl want to go?

1 _____

2 _____

3 _____

Where does the boy have to go?

1 _____

2 _____

3 _____

**LOOK!**

A:43

| I want to go to the park. | He/She wants to go to the park. |
| I have to go to the library. | He/She has to go to the library. |

**9** A:44 **Listen, circle, and match. Then say.**

She has to go to the dentist.

1 want to / have to  a

2 want to / have to  b

3 want to / have to  c

4 want to / have to  d

5 want to / have to  e

6 want to / have to  f

**10** **Look at Activity 9 and write.**

1 She has to go to the dentist.

2 _____

3 _____

4 _____

5 _____

6 _____

**From:** alex@yoohoo.com

**To:** sun_kwan@nmail.com

Hi Sun-kwan,

I'm writing to you because I want to have an online friend in a big city! I love sending emails to friends.

I live in a village on Sark. Sark is a very small British island, near France. Only 600 people live on Sark. I'm happy here because my family and friends are here. I love school, too. There's only one school on Sark and we sometimes play sports but often there aren't many people to make teams.

The beaches here are very clean and they're very quiet. There are two banks but there aren't any shopping malls on the island. We have to go by boat for an hour to another island to go shopping! On Sark, there isn't an airport and there aren't any cars. We ride our bikes everywhere. It's really quiet here.

I want to make new friends from different places. Do you like living in Seoul?

Please email me soon. I want to know about your life in a big city!

Alex

**12**  **Circle T = True or F = False.**

1 Alex loves emailing his friends.      T / F

2 Sark is a quiet island.      T / F

3 Alex doesn't like the island.      T / F

4 There is a shopping mall on the island.      T / F

5 You can fly to Sark.      T / F

**13** **Some sentences in Activity 12 are false. Write the correct sentences.**

1 _____

2 _____

3 _____

**14**  **Read. Where are the places in the photos?**

# Cool places

There are some very interesting cities, towns, and villages in the world. Here are some of them. Which do you want to see?

### Barcelona, Spain

Look at these beautiful chimneys! They are on the roof of a house in Barcelona. They are by Antoni Gaudi. Gaudi was a famous Spanish architect.

This is a nice place to sit, but it is noisy in the summer. It is in a big park and it looks like a snake! Its name is the Serpentine Bench.

### Bourton-on-the-Hill and Bourton-on-the-Water, England

One of these villages is on a hill and the other is on a river. In Bourton-on-the-Water, there are little bridges over the river. There are a lot of lovely old villages in England. They are usually quiet but beautiful.

### Alice Springs, Australia

Alice Springs is a town in the middle of the desert. A lot of tourists want to visit Alice Springs because the world-famous Ayers Rock is near the town.

**15**  **Circle.**

1  The chimneys by Antoni Gaudi are in (  Spain  /  the United Kingdom  ).

2  The Serpentine Bench is (  next to a museum  /  in a park  ).

3  Bourton-on-the-Water is (  on a river  /  next to the sea  ).

4  Alice Springs is (  a rock  /  a town  ).

5  Ayers Rock is in (  Australia  /  England  ).

**THINK**

Name an interesting city, town, or village in your country. Give reasons for your choice.

**16**  **Which place do you want to go to? Tell a friend.**

I want to go to Alice Springs because ….

 **MINI-PROJECT** Find a place that interests you. Write about it and share your article with the class.

**18**  **Why are there no animals on Future Island? Discuss your answers.**

**Circle T = True or F = False.**

1 Marta and Chris's new friend takes them to her house.     T / F

2 Food comes in bags.     T / F

3 The dog is a real dog.     T / F

4 Zero Zendell is the only person who has animals.     T / F

5 The zoo is Zero Zendell's zoo.     T / F

6 Champ is in the zoo.     T / F

 **Role-play the story.**

 **How flexible are you? Rank 1 to 5. Then share with a friend.**

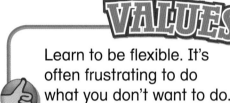

VALUES

Learn to be flexible. It's often frustrating to do what you don't want to do.

| Situation | A | B | C | D | E |
|---|---|---|---|---|---|
| | You want to play video games, but you have to do homework. | You want to go to a party, but you have to be home before 10 p.m. | You want to meet your friends, but you have to study before a test. | You want to stay up late, but you have to get up early. | You want to meet friends, but you have to take care of your little brother. |
| You | | | | | |
| Your friend | | | | | |

1 OK     2 not very frustrating     3 quite frustrating     4 frustrating     5 very frustrating

You want to play video games, but you have to do homework.

I think it's very frustrating. What about you?

HOME-SCHOOL LINK

Tell your family how to be flexible about things.

PARENT

**Where do you want to go?**

**1** Read the hints.

Z is the first letter.  A is between B and C.  D is between E and F.
G is next to I.  J is between K and L.  M is between N and O.
P is between R and S.  V is between U and X.  W is the last letter.

**2** Write the letters.

| A | B | C | D | E | F | G | H | I | J | K | L | M | N | O | P | Q | R | S | T | U | V | W | X | Y | Z |
|---|---|---|---|---|---|---|---|---|---|---|---|---|---|---|---|---|---|---|---|---|---|---|---|---|---|
| 1 | 2 | 3 | 4 | 5 | 6 | 7 | 8 | 9 | 10 | 11 | 12 | 13 | 14 | 15 | 16 | 17 | 18 | 19 | 20 | 21 | 22 | 23 | 24 | 25 | 26 |
| B |   | C | E |   | F | H | I |   | K |   | L | N |   | O | Q | R |   | S | T | U |   | X | Y |   |   |

**3** Change the numbers to letters.

| 19 | 16 | 20 | 21 | 16 | 7 | 7 | 9 | 4 | 5 |
|----|----|----|----|----|---|---|---|---|---|
| 20 | 13 | 4 | 21 | 8 | 9 | 20 | 2 | 20 | 20 |
| 4 | 9 | 3 | 2 | 16 | 21 | 21 | 16 | 26 | 8 |
| 8 | 2 | 20 | 3 | 20 | 18 | 3 | 16 | 9 | 16 |
| 16 | 18 | 21 | 11 | 19 | 3 | 6 | 11 | 15 | 19 |
| 16 | 3 | 13 | 5 | 9 | 19 | 9 | 20 | 15 | 19 |
| 13 | 18 | 5 | 18 | 21 | 3 | 22 | 21 | 9 | 9 |
| 15 | 25 | 5 | 25 | 3 | 18 | 15 | 16 | 14 | 14 |
| 2 | 3 | 14 | 11 | 13 | 11 | 5 | 18 | 10 | 10 |
| 20 | 21 | 3 | 21 | 9 | 16 | 14 | 5 | 19 | 15 |
| 16 | 3 | 9 | 18 | 19 | 16 | 18 | 21 | 16 | 3 |
| 7 | 3 | 4 | 21 | 16 | 18 | 25 | 8 | 16 | 13 |
| 5 | 3 | 18 | 4 | 3 | 6 | 5 | 23 | 13 | 13 |
| 18 | 5 | 20 | 21 | 3 | 22 | 18 | 3 | 14 | 21 |

**4** Find and cross out the place names i.e. ~~school.~~

**5** Write the letters that are left over: _____

**6** Unscramble these letters. Where do you want to go? _____

**23** (A:48) **Listen and number.**
**Then look and write.**

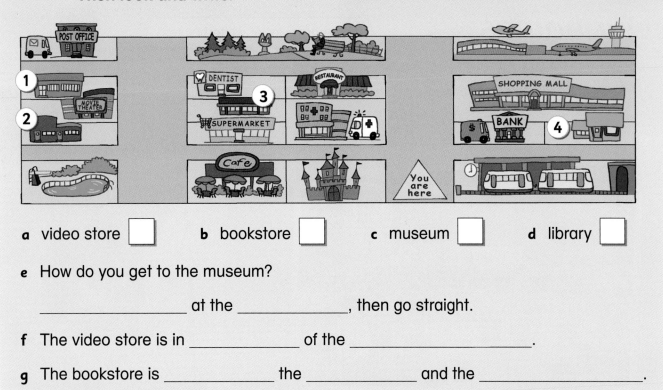

**a** video store ☐    **b** bookstore ☐    **c** museum ☐    **d** library ☐

**e** How do you get to the museum?

_____ at the _____, then go straight.

**f** The video store is in _____ of the _____.

**g** The bookstore is _____ the _____ and the _____.

**h** Where's the library? It's _____ the dentist.

---

**24**  **Unscramble and write. Then number.**

**a** have / I / to / supermarket / to / go / the

_____ ☐

**b** to / swimming / want / go / I

_____ ☐

**c** to / library / have / the / go / to / I

_____ ☐

**d** to / watch / I / movie / a / want

_____ ☐

**1** I have to get something for dinner.

**2** Yes, you do. You must take the books back before tomorrow.

**3** Can I come too? What time does it start?

**4** I want to do some exercise.

---

**I CAN**    I can say where a place is and how to get there. ☐

I can talk about what I want to do and what I have to do. ☐

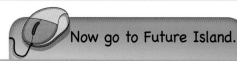 Now go to Future Island.

# Wider world 2
## Our homes

There are a lot of white houses.

**1**  Look at photos a–c and make sentences.

**2** A:49 Listen and read. Then number.

a

b

**1**

I'm from a small town in Andalucia, Spain. My house is very unusual. It's a cave house. Some people think caves are scary and dark but I think they're great. There are a lot of nice places to visit in my town. A lot of people go to the beautiful beaches on the weekend. It's fun to play volleyball on the sand. The old castles near my house are very interesting, too. My favorite is called Velez-Blanco. I love my home!

Alba, 11, Spain

**2**

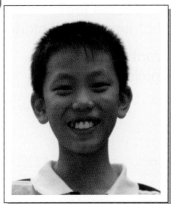

I live in Hong Kong, a very busy place in China. Seven million people live in Hong Kong. It's very noisy here but it's never boring. I live on the fortieth floor of a building in Kowloon. It has great views. There's a sports center behind our apartment. I go there every day to learn taekwondo. There are a lot of shopping malls, restaurants, and museums near my home. The science museum is my favorite. I always learn new and interesting things there. I love Hong Kong!

Chiu-Wai, 12, China

c

## 3

I live on an island in Greece called Paros. I live with my family in a beautiful white house in a village. The island is quite small—just 13,000 people live here. There's a harbor near our house. My sister and I like going there and watching the boats. We like sailing and sometimes we go fishing with our father. My father loves fishing but he's not very good! I love living on an island.

Eleni, 12, Greece

**3**  **Circle.**

**1** Alba lives in a ( cave house / beach house ) in Spain.

**2** She likes going to the ( museum / beach ) on the weekend.

**3** There's a ( supermarket / sports center ) behind Chiu-Wai's apartment.

**4** Chiu-Wai is learning ( taekwondo / sailing ).

**5** Eleni lives ( near a river / on an island ).

**6** Eleni's father is ( not good at / good at ) fishing.

**4**  **Ask and answer.**

**1** Where do you want to live and why?

**2** What do you like about where you live?

**3** What don't you like about where you live?

## YOUR TURN!

Draw your ideal town or city. Then write about it.

What's the town's name?
Where is it?
What does it look like?
What's it like living there?
What are your favorite places?

ⓐ movie theater
ⓑ sports center
ⓒ swimming pool
ⓓ museum

# Good days and bad days

**1** (A:50) **Listen and read. Is Tom happy?**

**2** (A:51) **Listen and say.**

a. curry
b. an omelet
c. spaghetti
d. fish and chips
e. paella
f. dumplings
g. sushi
h. stew
i. rice and beans

**3** **Do you like the food in Activity 2? Ask and answer.**

**A:** Do you like curry?     **B:** Yes, I love it!

*International food dishes*

**4** (A:53) **Listen and number the events in order. Then say.**

## LOOK!

(A:52)

| | |
|---|---|
| I cooked stew. | He dropped the plate. |
| She paddled very quickly. | We fell in the lake. |

Hannah cooked omelets.

**5** **Look at Activity 4 and write.**

**1** Maria _____.

**2** Tom _____.

**3** They _____.

**4** Hannah _____.

**5** They _____.

**6** 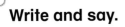 **Write and say.**

climbed   fell
wanted   sailed   dropped

**1** Yesterday, I _____ a plate in the kitchen.

**2** Last week, we _____ new bikes but my mom said "No!"

**3** A year ago, he _____ Mount Everest.

**4** In 2004, she _____ around the world.

**5** Last month, I _____ in the river when I was fishing.

**7**  **Talk to a friend about last week.**

I cooked fish and chips!

**8** A:54 **Listen and say.**

a
**pack my bag**

b
**miss the bus**

c
**pass a test**

d
**eat my lunch**

e
**bring my juice**

f
**drop the ball**

**9** A:55-56 **Listen to the song and write.**

**Chorus:**
*It was a bad day, it was really bad.*
*But you smiled at me, now I'm not sad.*

I _____ my school bag and walked up the street.
I _____ the bus, "Ow, my tired feet."
I didn't _____ my test, I was late for class.
My friends said, "Next time, get here fast."
I opened my lunchbox, and said, "No way!"
I didn't _____ my juice today.

**(Chorus)**
I went to the park and played with a ball.
I kicked it too hard, it went over a wall.
A boy helped me, he didn't say his name.
We played baseball in the park and enjoyed the game.
I _____ the ball, he said, "That's OK."
Now he's my new friend and it was a good day.

**10**  **Look at Activity 9 and circle T = True or F = False.**

1  She didn't miss the bus.                    T / F

2  She was late for class.                     T / F

3  She brought her juice.                      T / F

4  She didn't kick a ball.                     T / F

5  She played badminton in the park.           T / F

**11** **In Activity 10, four sentences are false. Say the true sentences.**

## LOOK!

A:57

| What happened? | I didn't pass my test because I didn't study. |
| --- | --- |
| | He didn't bring his juice because he was late for school. |

**12** 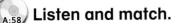 **Write and say.**

1 We _____ because we were sad. (not laugh)

2 She _____ her eyes because it was a scary movie. (not open)

3 They _____ a second soccer game because they weren't tired. (play)

4 I _____ the test because I studied a lot. (pass)

5 He _____ the bus because he was early. (not miss)

**13** A:58 **Listen and match.**

**1** Jenny    **2** Jackie and Kari    **3** Miki and Sam    **4** Mike    **5** Ken and Rob

**14**  **Look at Activity 13 and write.**

1 She _____ the ball because the sun was in her eyes.

2 They _____ the test because they didn't study.

3 They _____ in the sea because there was a red flag.

4 He _____ the curry because he doesn't like spicy food.

5 They _____ soccer because it was too hot.

**15**  **Ask and answer.**
**What didn't you do? Why?**

I didn't play soccer because I was tired.

**16**  A:59 **Read. Then number.**

# My good day

**1**

One Saturday last May was a great day for me. I played the guitar in a school concert. I was scared. I didn't want to play. Then I went on stage and I was OK. I really liked it! Now I want to be a rock star!

Jake, 12

**2**

My cousin's wedding last year was wonderful. There were a lot of people—about a hundred! The food was great. There was some tasty fish and a tall cake. I didn't want to wear a pink dress but it looked good on me. Now pink is my favorite color!

Laura, 13

**3**

Last Friday was a really good day. After school, I went to the park with my friends and we played basketball. Then, a group of girls from another school joined us and we played together. It was fun!

Sandy, 12

**17** **Circle T = True or F = False. Then say.**

| | | |
|---|---|---|
| **1** Jake wanted to play on stage. | T / F | |
| **2** Jake played the guitar. | T / F | *False! He didn't want to play on stage.* |
| **3** There was curry at the wedding. | T / F | |
| **4** Laura didn't want to wear a pink dress. | T / F | |
| **5** Sandy played soccer in the park last Friday. | T / F | |
| **6** A group of girls from Sandy's school joined her. | T / F | |

**18** **Correct the false sentences from Activity 17.**

1 _____

2 _____

3 _____

4 _____

**19**  **Read. What did Ellen do in 2005?**

## Amazing Ellen

**1** Ellen MacArthur is a British sailor who sailed alone in a race around the world. The race started in November 2004 and she finished in February 2005. She was the first woman across the finish line. In the seventy-two days Ellen was at sea, she filmed her journey. There were good and bad days and on her videos we can see them.

**2** It was often dangerous but Ellen was brave. There were storms and the waves were very big. Her food was boring and dry and she was often tired. One very bad day for Ellen was Christmas Day. There was a big storm and it was scary. Ellen phoned her family but she didn't want to talk. She was sad and cried. She didn't open her Christmas presents.

**3** New Year's Day was good for Ellen. There were no storms. Ellen phoned her friends and family. She opened her Christmas presents, seven days late, and smiled and laughed. There were some funny presents. One present was chocolate and she loved it. She enjoyed that day.

**20**  **Choose a title for each paragraph. Number.**

**1** Ellen the sailor ☐     **2** A good day ☐     **3** A bad day ☐

**21**  **Circle.**

**1** The race started in ( November / December ) 2004.

**2** The race finished in ( 2005 / 2006 ).

**3** It was ( never / often ) dangerous.

**4** Ellen ( enjoyed / didn't enjoy ) Christmas Day 2004.

**5** Ellen ( phoned / didn't phone ) her family on New Year's Day.

**22** 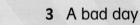 **Ask and answer.**

**1** Do you like sailing?        **2** What sports do you like?

**3** Do you want to be a sportsperson?

### THINK

Make a list of good and bad things that happened to you yesterday. Was it a good day or a bad day?

### MINI-PROJECT

Find out about a famous sportsperson. Write a profile and share it with the class.

 **Listen and read.**

  **Why does Serena say Champ is having a wild time? Discuss your answers.**

**25**   **Circle T = True or F = False.**

1 Marta and Chris went inside the zoo.  T / F

2 Cameras and dogs are guarding the zoo.  T / F

3 A guard saw Serena on camera.  T / F

4 The guards didn't lock Champ's cage.  T / F

5 Champ opened the cage door.  T / F

6 Champ is all right.  T / F

**26**  **Role-play the story.**

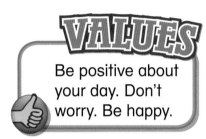

**VALUES**

Be positive about your day. Don't worry. Be happy.

**27**  **How do you relax after a bad day?**
**Write *always*, *often*, *sometimes*, or *never*.**
**Then ask and answer.**

|  | You | Your friend |
|---|---|---|
| 1 Practice a sport. |  |  |
| 2 Watch TV or play video games. |  |  |
| 3 Go online and talk to a friend. |  |  |
| 4 Write a blog post describing your day. |  |  |
| 5 Talk to a family member. |  |  |
| 6 Other? |  |  |

I always go online and talk to a friend. What about you?

I often go online and talk to a friend but I always talk to a family member.

**HOME-SCHOOL LINK**

Ask your family members how they relax after a bad day. PARENT

yesterday   last week   last month   last year   an hour ago   two days ago

**FINISH**

**28** missed

**27** Did you brush your teeth?

**26**

**25** played

**20**

**21** climbed

**22** Did you wash the dishes?

**23** got

**24** Did you do your homework?

**19** made

**18** ate

**17**

**16**

**15** Did you get up late?

**10** Did you miss the bus?

**11**

**12** Did you help your friend?

**13** Did you make your bed yesterday?

**14** brought

**9** drank

**8**

**7**

**6** went

**5**

**START**

**1** wrote

**2** saw

**3** Did you take out the garbage?

**4** dropped

If there is a word in the box, use it to say a sentence with a time phrase.
If there is a question, answer the question by rolling the dice:
1, 2, 3 (no) and 4, 5, 6 (yes).
Think about the answer.
If it is good on a ladder ("Did you take out the garbage?" "Yes, I did.") go up.
If it is bad on a slide ("Did you help your friend?" "No, I didn't.") go down.

I wrote some poetry yesterday.

**PROGRESS CHECK** **4**

What happened?

| | a | b | c |
|---|---|---|---|
| **1** Mandy | ☐ | ☐ | ☐ |
| **2** Greg | ☐ | ☐ | ☐ |
| **3** Eric | ☐ | ☐ | ☐ |
| **4** Joan | ☐ | ☐ | ☐ |

**30** **Write.**

> sushi    omelet    curry    stew    wrote    made    drank    ate

I like cooking. I went to a cooking school last year. I cooked many kinds of dishes at the school. After making dishes we [1] _____ how to make them in our notebooks. I [2] _____ a Spanish dish called paella. It had rice and seafood in it. I also made an [3] _____. It's made from eggs.

My favorite dishes are hot and spicy. When I go out to a restaurant, I always order [4] _____. It's a very popular food in India and some Asian countries. On my birthday, I [5] _____ a really hot curry and [6] _____ about two liters of water!

I like other kinds of food, too. For example, I like [7] _____. It's made with rice and raw fish. It's from Japan. Other foods I like are dumplings, fish and chips, and many different types of [8] _____. Some of these are vegetarian and some have beef or chicken in them.

**I CAN**
I can talk about food from different countries. ☐
I can say what happened and didn't happen in the past. ☐

**TEACHER**

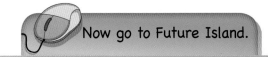 Now go to Future Island.

# Review Units 3 and 4

**1**  **Ask and answer. You are in the music store.**

1  How do I get to the station?
2  I want to go to the movie theater. Where is it?
3  How do I get to the supermarket?
4  I want to go to the swimming pool. Where is it?
5  How do I get to the library?
6  I want to go to the children's park. Where is it?

**2**  **Choose three more places on the map. Ask and answer.**

**3**  **Write. Then say.**

1  she / want / station

_____

2  they / have / swimming pool

_____

3  he / want / hospital

_____

She wants to go to the station.

**4**  **Write about yourself.**

1  What do you have to do today?

_____

2  What do you want to do today?

_____

**5** Look and write.

INTERNATIONAL FOOD FAIR

1 _____
2 _____
3 _____
4 _____
5 _____
6 _____
7 _____

**6** Imagine you are at the food fair. Write. Then say.

First, I want to eat _____ .

Second, I want to eat _____ .

Third, I want to eat _____ .

**7** Write the opposite.

1 I liked the movie last night.

I didn't like the movie last night.

2 He didn't climb a mountain last year.

_____

3 Yesterday, we didn't stay at the library all afternoon.

_____

4 James visited his grandparents last Saturday.

_____

5 Sally didn't walk to school yesterday.

_____

6 We played soccer in the park last weekend.

_____

# Trips

**1** B:02 **Listen and read. Did they enjoy today?**

**1** Hi! Did you enjoy the trip today? Did you like the palace?

Yes, I did. It was great.

Yes, I'll write about the palace for my history homework.

Good idea, Tom. Here are four tickets for the amusement park tomorrow.

**2** Maria, how about you? What did you do today?

I went to the palace, too, and then the museum. It was really interesting.

Great. I'll go get Felipe and you can talk about tomorrow.

**3** Hi, Felipe. We're planning tomorrow now. What will you do at the amusement park?

I think I'll go on the water slide first.

Yeah, me too!

**2** B:03 **Listen and say.**

**a**  aquarium

**b**  amusement park

**c**  palace

**d**  water park

**e**  theater

**f**  national park

**g**  circus

**3**  **Look at Activity 1. Where did Flo, Tom, and Maria go?**

*Tourist attractions*

## LOOK!

| What did you do yesterday? | I went to the aquarium. |
| Did you go to the aquarium? | Yes, I did. / No, I didn't. |
| Did you like the aquarium? | |

**4**  **Listen and circle.**

1  Did Maria go to Buckingham Palace?     Yes, she did.  /  No, she didn't.

2  Did Maria go to the aquarium?     Yes, she did.  /  No, she didn't.

3  Did Maria go to the theater?     Yes, she did.  /  No, she didn't.

4  Did Maria go to an Indian restaurant?     Yes, she did.  /  No, she didn't.

**5**  **Stick and circle. Then ask and answer.**

Stick

| | | | |
|---|---|---|---|
| **1** I went to the …. | | | |
| **2** Did you like the …? | ✓ / ✗ | ✓ / ✗ | ✓ / ✗ |
| **3** I didn't go to the …. | | | |

Did you go to the museum?
Yes, I did.

Did you like the museum?
Yes, I did.

**6**  **Ask and answer. What did you do yesterday?**

Did you go to the park?
No, I didn't.

**7** B:06 **Listen and say.**

**a** ride the Ferris wheel

**b** go on the bumper cars

**c** play miniature golf

**d** ride the carousel

**e** go on the paddle boats

**f** ride the roller coaster

**g** go on the pirate ship

**h** go on the water slide

**8** B:07-08 **Listen to the song and write.**

SONG

We went to an _____ yesterday.
A special treat for my brother's birthday.
Did you like the _____, going up high?
Yes, I did! Because I can fly!

Did you like the _____ with horses of gold?
No, we didn't! The horses were small and we're too old!
Did you like the _____ then, fun and fast?
No, we didn't! Our car was slow and we were last.

So what rides did you like? Did you enjoy your trip?
Did you like the _____ and the _____?
Yes, and we loved the _____, it was so quick.
We went on it ten times and now we feel sick!

**9** **Look and say.**

**1** Did he play basketball last week?

**2** Did they like the carousel?

**3** Did we play miniature golf last week?

**4** Did she like the paddle boats?

What will you do at the amusement park?

First, I'll ride the Ferris wheel. Then, I'll go on the bumper cars.

**10** **Listen and number. Then ask and answer.**

What will you do at the amusement park?

First, I'll ride the carousel. Then, I'll go on the pirate ship.

1 **a**

**b**

2 **a**

**b**

3 **a**

**b**

**11** **Look at Activity 10 and write.**

1 First, I'll _____.

Then, I'll _____.

2 First, _____.

Then, _____.

3 _____

_____

**12**  **Ask and answer. What will you do next week/summer/winter/year?**

**13**   **Read. Then match the underlined words to the photos.**

# Hawaii is the place to be!

a

Fantastic <u>sandy beaches (1)</u>, great sea, and lots to do! Go <u>surfing (2)</u>, sailing, or <u>paragliding (3)</u>!

Visit the Waikiki Aquarium or the Wet 'n' Wild water park! At night, see a concert or try <u>Hawaiian dancing (4)</u>!

There's something for the whole family!

b

c

d

*August 14th*

Hi Gemma,
I'm in Hawaii. It's great! On the first day we went surfing. The sea was warm but surfing was difficult. I'll try it again tomorrow. We also went paragliding. It was exciting flying in the air! Yesterday it rained but today it was hot and it didn't rain. We played volleyball on the beach.
The aquarium was good and I really loved the sea turtles and the fish. We also visited the water park.
It was a great vacation and I want to come back next year. Are you enjoying your summer vacation, too? What did you do? Where did you go? I'll see you when I get back.
Love,
Sarah

**14** **Write.**

**1** What water activities can you do in Hawaii?

_____

**2** When can you try Hawaiian dancing?

_____

**3** What was the weather like in Hawaii yesterday?

_____

**4** When did Sarah go surfing?

_____

**15**  **Talk about your last vacation and your plan for your next vacation.**

I went to the beach last summer, and in the winter I'll go skiing.

**16** B:12 **Read. What do the different flags mean?**

SOCIAL SCIENCE 5

SEARCH

# BEACH SAFETY IN AUSTRALIA

a

b

## Sun safety

- Slip on some clothes—always wear a T-shirt or other clothes.
- Slop on the sunblock—always wear sunblock in the sun.
- Slap on a hat—always wear a hat to cover your head in the sun.

### Slip, slop, slap!

## Swim safety

- Swim between the red and yellow flags. This water is safe.
- Never swim near a red flag. It means the water is dangerous.
- Always swim near the beach. Don't swim far away.

c

## Surf safety

- Always surf between the surfing signs.
- Always stay with your surfboard.
- Never surf between blue flags.

**17** **Look at Activity 16 and write.**

1 You can't surf between _____ flags.

2 The water is _____ between the yellow and red flags.

3 You can't swim near a _____ flag.

4 Wear a hat to _____ your head.

5 Slop on the _____.

## THINK!

Safety instructions are sometimes in two or more languages? Why?

 MINI-**PROJECT** Find out about beach safety in your country and make a poster.

Cross-curricular

*Social science: Beach safety*

65

STORY

**1** What can we do? How can we rescue Champ?

It's difficult ....

**2** Wait! I know this place! Isn't it the nature reserve?

What? Here?

Yes, I'll check the sign.

**3** THE LAST NATURE RESERVE ON THE ISLAND WAS HERE
IT CLOSED 100 YEARS AGO

**4** My parents started this nature reserve. There was an underground river!

Where?

**5** Here! It was easy to bring food for the animals ... we used the river!

Where did it go?

It went from the harbor, past the zoo, and into the nature reserve!

NATURE RESERVE
ZOO
HARBOR

**6** Cool! It's the river!

Yes! And we can use it! We can get into Zero Zendell's Zoo!

And then we'll rescue Champ!

19 **How does Marta know about the river? Discuss your answers.**

**20** Circle T = True or F = False.

1 It is easy to rescue Champ.       T / F

2 The nature reserve closed 200 years ago.       T / F

3 Marta's parents started the nature reserve and used the river to bring food for the animals.       T / F

4 Marta looks for the river in the ground.       T / F

5 The river goes from the harbor to the nature reserve.       T / F

6 The children can use the river to get to the zoo.       T / F

**21**  Role-play the story.

**22**  Write in the schedule below to plan your day. Then share with a friend.

## VALUES
Plan, but be flexible. Planning helps you do more things.

> do my homework    meet my friends    call a friend
> go online to Future Island    update my blog

### Saturday

| Time | To do | How long? |
|------|-------|-----------|
| 7:30 | get up, shower, and have breakfast | 1 hour |
| | | |
| | | |
| | | |
| | | |

> I think I will get up, shower, and have breakfast at 7:30.

> I will get up, shower, and have breakfast at 7:00.

### HOME-SCHOOL LINK

Help a family member to plan his/her day.

PARENT

**Stick. Then listen to your friend and stick.**

## Design an amusement park!

Your amusement park

Your friend's amusement park

The Ferris wheel is next to the entrance.

**Listen and check (✓).**

Last week

Next week

**1** **a**   **b**   Monday

**2** **a**   **b**

**3** **a**   **b**   Tuesday

**4** **a** 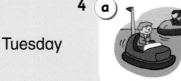  **b**

**5** **a**   **b**   Wednesday

**6** **a**   **b**

**7** **a**   **b**   Thursday

**8** **a**   **b**

**9** **a**   **b**   Friday

**10** **a**   **b**

 **Look at Activity 24 and write.**

**1** What did she do last Monday? _____

**2** What will she do next Tuesday? _____

**3** What did she do last Wednesday? _____

**4** What did she do last Thursday? _____

**5** What will she do next Friday? _____

 I can talk about the places I went to.

I can talk about what I will do in the future.

 TEACHER

Now go to Future Island.

# Wider world 3
## Our vacations

This place is in the mountains. It looks like an old town.

 1 Look at photos a–c and make sentences.

a

b

 2 B:15 Listen and read. Then number.

**1**

Last year, I went to a city called Agra in India. I visited the Taj Mahal (1) with my family. A man called Emperor Shah Jahan married a princess called Mumtaz Mahal. When she died he was very sad. He built the Taj Mahal for her. Twenty thousand workers used one thousand elephants and finished it in 1653. The tombs of Emperor Shah Jahan and his wife are inside the Taj Mahal. I think the Taj Mahal is beautiful!

Samir, 11, India

**2**

This summer, I went by bus to an ancient city in Turkey called Cappadocia. We stayed in a hotel in front of the Uchisar Castle. During the day, we visited a city that was inside a mountain. There are houses, restaurants, and hotels all inside the mountain. We then went in a hot-air balloon and saw the beautiful Fairy Chimneys (2). After that, we visited a famous Turkish bath. I can't wait to visit Cappadocia again next year.

Zara, 12, Turkey

c

3

**Circle T = True or F = False.**

1 The Taj Mahal is in India.                          T / F

2 There aren't any tombs inside
the Taj Mahal.                                        T / F

3 Zara's hotel was inside a castle.                    T / F

4 You can visit a Turkish bath at
Cappadocia.                                           T / F

5 People called Andes lived in
Machu Picchu long ago.                                T / F

6 The Intihuatana Stone was a sundial.  T / F

4 **Ask and answer.**

1 What was your favorite vacation?
2 What's a nice place to visit where you live?

3

Last year, I visited a city called **Machu Picchu (3)**. It's in the Andes mountains in Peru. Long ago, people called Incas lived in this ancient city. The city was lost in the mountains for hundreds of years. There are ruins of gardens, houses, and even a palace. My favorite ruin is called the Intihuatana Stone. It was a big sundial at the top of a big pyramid. There were often special celebrations around the Intihuatana Stone. Machu Picchu is a great place to visit!

Juan, 12, Peru

## YOUR TURN!

**Ask and answer in your class. Present the results in a graph.**

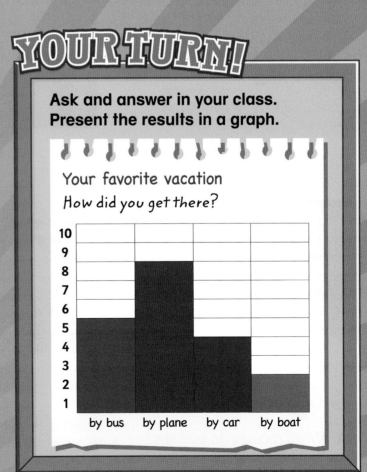

Your favorite vacation
How did you get there?

# 6 Arts and entertainment

**1** B:16 **Listen and read. What is Shadow in the House?**

**1** Hi, Maria!

Hi guys! I just saw Shadow in the House by myself. It's a scary thriller, but I had a great time!

**2** Hello!

There was something in the house. It wrote letters on the window ...

**3** ... and it made terrible noises ....

**4** Boo! Aaah! Flo, we didn't see you!

**5** Sorry, Maria!

**2** B:17 **Listen and say.**

**a** thriller

**b** comedy

**c** sci-fi

**d** romance

**e** musical

**f** cartoon

**3** **Ask and answer.**

**A:** What movies do you like?
**B:** I like thrillers and ....

**4**  **Look at Activity 1. Circle T = True or F = False.**

1 Maria saw a scary movie.    T / F

2 Maria didn't have a good time.    T / F

3 The shadow didn't write on the window.    T / F

4 The shadow made friendly noises.    T / F

5 Flo didn't make a scary noise.    T / F

B:18
## LOOK!

| |
|---|
| I saw the movie by myself. |
| You wrote it by yourself. |
| He made it by himself. |
| She didn't go to the movie by herself. |
| We didn't watch it by ourselves. |
| They didn't draw it by themselves. |

**5** (B:19) **Circle. Then listen and check your answers.**

1

I ( wrote / didn't write ) the letter by myself.

2

The girl ( played / didn't play ) by herself.

3

They ( made / didn't make ) dinner by themselves.

4

He ( watched / didn't watch ) the movie by himself.

**6**  **Write. Then say.**

I wrote my homework last Monday by myself.

1 I _____ my homework last Monday _____. (write/me)

2 You _____ a movie last week _____. (see/you)

3 We _____ a good time last Saturday _____. (have/we)

4 He _____ dinner for his family yesterday _____. (make/he)

5 They _____ karaoke last year _____. (sing/they)

**7** B:20-21 **Listen and say. Then listen to the music and number the instrument.**

a

b harmonica ☐

c

d triangle ☐

e drums ☐

saxophone ☐

cello ☐

f

g

h

clarinet ☐

harp ☐

tambourine ☐

**8** B:22 **Listen and say. Do you know any other types of music?**

a jazz    b rock    c blues    d pop    e country

**9** B:23-24 **Listen to the song and write.**

SONG

Chorus:

*Did you hear the music last night on the radio? (x2)*

I didn't feel happy, I was so sad.
But the music was great. It made me feel glad.

(Chorus)

Yes, I did. Playing funky _____

was a _____.

And I loved dancing to it on my own.

(Chorus)

No, I didn't. Was it _____?

Was it _____?

What was it like?

_____ music with guitars
and violins. It was all right.

(Chorus)

Yes, I did. It was the kind of
music I choose—guitar and
_____ playing the blues.

**10** B:23 **Listen to the song again and circle.**

1  Did you hear the guitar?          Y / N
2  Did you hear the saxophone?   Y / N
3  Did you hear the violin?            Y / N
4  Did you hear the harmonica?   Y / N
5  Did you hear the piano?           Y / N

**11** **Ask and answer.**

1  see / a concert / last week?
2  make / a cake / on Sunday?
3  say sorry / yesterday?
4  have / a party / last month?
5  sing / a song / last night?

| B:25 | |
|---|---|
| Did you hear the cello? | Yes, I did. / No, I didn't. |
| Have you ever played the saxophone? | Yes, I have. / No, I haven't. |
| Have you ever been to a concert? | Yes, I have. / No, I've never been to a concert. |

**12**  **Listen and check (✓).**

**1**
a
b

**2**
a
b

**TIP!**

play    played
go      been
got     gotten
eat     eaten

*See more on p. 115.*

**3**
a
b

**4**
a
b

**13**  **Look at Activity 12 and write the questions and your answers. Then ask and answer.**

1 Have you _____ 100 per cent in a test?

Your answer: _____

2 Have _____?

Your answer: _____

3 _____ to another country?

Your answer: _____

4 _____ in one day?

Your answer: _____

**14**   **Read. Is the book a thriller, a romance, or a comedy?**

SEARCH

# Diary of a Wimpy Kid

I love this book. I read it every day last summer. It's about a boy, Greg. Greg is a normal boy in middle school and he writes in a diary (he says it's a "journal") every day. Greg has a best friend, Rowley, and a mean little brother.

I don't think Greg is wimpy. He's really brave and clever. There are some funny events. My favorite part is the story at Halloween. One day, Greg and Rowley argue and they aren't friends anymore. Greg is friends with his neighbor for some time and doesn't speak to Rowley. The ending is good, but I can't tell you!

The book was really funny and it made me laugh a lot. I loved the cartoon pictures in the book, too. I liked it because I'm in middle school too— and my best friend's name is Greg. He's like the Wimpy Kid!

Krishan, 13

DIARY
of a
Wimpy Kid

a novel
in cartoons

INTERNATIONAL
BESTSELLER

Jeff Kinney

**15**  **Check (✓).**

**1** Wimpy means ….

  **a** brave and clever ☐    **b** not brave ☐    **c** normal ☐

**2** Krishan read the book ….

  **a** last week ☐    **b** last month ☐    **c** last summer ☐

**3** The two boys in the book were ….

  **a** Greg and Halloween ☐  **b** Greg and Rowley ☐  **c** Rowley and Krishan ☐

**4** The two boys were friends ….

  **a** all the time ☐    **b** most of the time ☐    **c** on the weekend ☐

**5** The book made Krishan ….

  **a** laugh a lot ☐    **b** smile a lot ☐    **c** jump a lot ☐

**16** **What is your favorite book? Discuss your answers.**

**1** Is it a comedy/thriller/romance?

**2** What are the characters like?

**3** Why do you like it?

My favorite book is ….

**17**  Read the poem. Match the questions to the pictures.

# Bad day

*By José Luis Morales*

On a bad day, bad things happen.
Have you ever failed a test?
Have you ever missed a bus?
Have you ever been afraid?
Have you ever fallen down?
Have you ever scraped your knee?
Have you ever hurt your foot?
Have you ever lost your keys?
Have you ever had a headache?
Have you ever felt real sad?
Have you ever missed a friend?
Have you ever said "That's bad!"?
On a bad day, bad things happen.
Take a deep breath. Count to ten.
Think a good day lies ahead.

**18** Have any of the things in the poem ever happened to you? How did you feel? What were you doing at the time?

**19**  Write the opposites.

| | |
|---|---|
| **1** fail a test | _____ a test |
| **2** miss a bus | _____ a bus |
| **3** lose your keys | _____ your keys |
| **4** feel sad | feel _____ |
| **5** That's bad! | That's _____! |

## THINK

What else should you do if you're having a bad day? Think of three more things.

**20**  Choose three questions from the poem. Ask and answer.

Have you ever been afraid?

Yes, I have. I was riding a roller coaster.

## MINI-
## PROJECT

Write a poem for this title: "Good day." Use the "Bad day" poem as a model. Start with: "On a good day, good things happen."

1

Hey look! Have you ever seen a flashing moon?

It's not the moon. It's the ads.

2

Yes, but ... oh right!

Friends!

3

Last year, I crossed the sea to Africa ....

4

I went into the dark jungle by myself.

5

And I saved the last chimpanzee in the world!

6

And I brought him here— to Zero Zendell's Zoo!

Zero's my hero!

7

That isn't true! He stole that chimp from me!!

Yes, we saw him!

22  **Why do the people of Future Island admire Zero Zendell? Discuss your answers.**

**23** **Write.**

1  Is the moon flashing? _____

2  Did Zero Zendell cross the sea to Africa? _____

3  Did Zero Zendell go into the dark jungle? _____

4  Did Zero Zendell save the last chimp? _____

5  Did Zero Zendell steal the chimp? _____

6  Did the people believe Zero Zendell? _____

**24**  **Role-play the story.**

**25**  **Read and write ✓ = by myself or ✓✓ = with my friends. Then share with a friend.**

Learn to be self-sufficient. You can always do some things by yourself.

| | You | Your friend |
|---|---|---|
| **1** Review for a test. | | |
| **2** Go to a concert. | | |
| **3** Make a draft for something you are writing. | | |
| **4** Do homework. | | |
| **5** Go to the movies. | | |
| **6** Find information for a project. | | |

I review for a test by myself.

I review for a test with my friends.

**HOME-SCHOOL LINK**

Tell your family about the things you can do by yourself.

PARENT

HAVE FUN!

**FINISH**

**17** Have you ever played the harp?

**16** Have you ever played in a band?

**15** What did you do yesterday by yourself?

**18** Have you ever been to a concert?

**12** Have you ever eaten popcorn at the movie theater?

**14** Have you ever made a birthday cake?

**11** Did you say "Good morning" today?

**13** Which do you like: a sci-fi movie, a romance, or a musical?

**9** Have you ever seen a musical at the theater?

**8** Have you ever been late for school?

**7** Have you ever watched a sci-fi movie?

**10** How was the weather yesterday?

**6** Did you eat all your lunch yesterday?
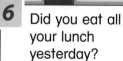

**1** Did you come to school today by yourself?

**2** Have you ever listened to an English song?

**3** Did you help your friends today?

**5** Have you ever listened to jazz?

**START**

**4** Which do you like: a comedy, a thriller, or a cartoon?

No, I didn't come by myself. I came to school today with my friend.

Have you ever ...?

| | | a | b | c |
|---|---|---|---|---|
| **1** | Ann | ☐ | ☐ | ☐ |
| **2** | Dave | ☐ | ☐ | ☐ |
| **3** | Jay | ☐ | ☐ | ☐ |
| **4** | Sarah | ☐ | ☐ | ☐ |

**28**   **Unscramble and write questions. Then number.**

> **1** Yes, I have. I did it last year.
> **2** No, I don't really like it.
> **3** Yes, I did. It sounded great.
> **4** No, I was busy doing my homework.

**a** you / hear / did / my / night / song / last / on / TV

_____ ☐

**b** hot / you / eaten / ever / very / curry / have

_____ ☐

**c** a / night / see / last / did / you / movie

_____ ☐

**d** run / have / kilometers / ever / ten / you

_____ ☐

**I CAN**
I can talk about who did something.  ☐
I can talk about what I have done.  ☐

TEACHER

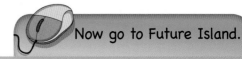
Now go to Future Island.

# Review *Units 5 and 6*

## 1 ✏️ Number. Then write.

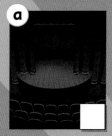 a
 b
 c
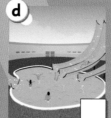 d
 e
 f

1  A king or queen lives here.  _____

2  We can see actors here.  _____

3  We can see a lot of fish here.  _____

4  We can see paintings and dinosaurs here.  _____

5  We can ride a roller coaster here.  _____

6  We can jump into the water here.  _____

## 2 💿 B:31 Listen and match. Where will the girl go?

| | | |
|---|---|---|
| 1 | First | aquarium |
| 2 | Second | museum |
| 3 | Third | circus |
| 4 | Fourth | palace |

## 3 💿 B:32 Listen and write Y = Yes or N = No.

 1
 2
 3
 4

## 4 ✏️ Unscramble. Then look at Activity 3 and circle T = True or F = False.

1  the / she / roller coaster / liked          T / F

2  playing / they / miniature golf / like / didn't          T / F

3  liked / she / Ferris wheel / the /          T / F

4  carousel / like / the / he / didn't          T / F

**5** 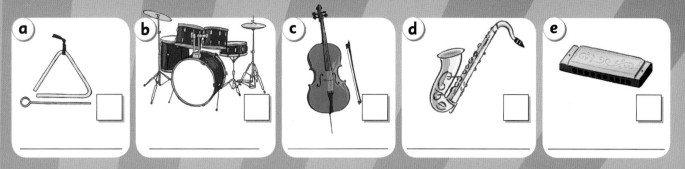 Listen and number. Then write.

a _____

b _____

c _____

d _____

e _____

**6** Listen and number.

**7** 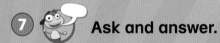 Ask and answer.

1 What did you do yesterday?
2 Did you … last summer?
3 Did you … by yourself?
4 Have you ever …?

**8** Complete the sentences.

1 Yesterday, I _____ by myself.

2 I have never _____ .

# Space

**1** B:35 **Listen and read. Can you see Tom and Flo?**

**2** B:36 **Listen and say.**

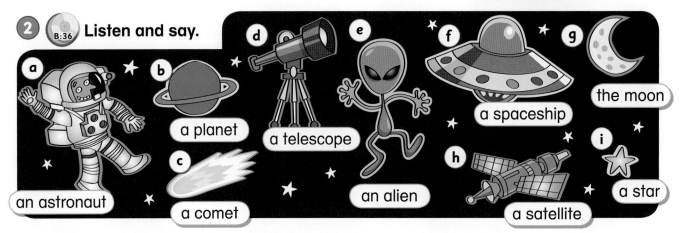

**3** **Look at Activity 1. Find and say the questions for these answers.**

1 I like to watch the stars at night.

2 Let me see.

3 Here.

4 It's Tom and Flo.

LOOK!

B:37

| Who are they? | They're astronauts. |
| When did they come? | They came last night. |
| Where did they come from? | They came from the moon. |
| How did they get here? | They came by spaceship. |
| Why are you looking at the sky? | I saw a flashing light. |
| What's that flashing light? | It's a spaceship. |

**4** B:38 **Listen. Then circle.**

**1** Where was Felipe in his dream?

a

b

c

**2** Why was he there?

a

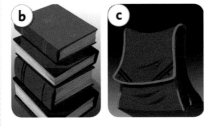
b   c

**3** What was the inside of the spaceship like?

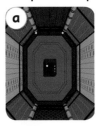
a

b

c

**5** **Look at the answers and write questions.**

1 She's my mom.   Who _____?

2 It's my birthday.   Why _____?

3 They're stars.   What _____?

4 It's next to the swimming pool.   Where _____?

5 At seven o'clock.   When _____?

**6** **Ask and answer.**

1 Who is your teacher?   2 Why are you happy/tired?

3 Where is your home?   4 What sports do you like?

5 When is your birthday?

**7**  B:39 **Listen and say.**

**a**
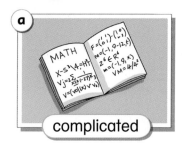
complicated

**b**

amazing

**c**

frightening

**d**

intelligent

**e**

brilliant

**f**

important

**8** B:40-41 **Listen to the song and write.**

Travel in space is _____ exciting,
Than travel on Earth below.
It's more _____, too, and more _____,
If you really want to know.

The question is—think about it,
Do _____ live out there?
And if they do, are they more _____,
Than humans everywhere?

I don't know all the answers,
But one thing I know is true,
That the world is an _____ place,
And it's just right for me and you, me and you.

## LOOK!

B:42

| Which telescope is more complicated? | The big telescope is more complicated than the small telescope. |
| --- | --- |
| Which telescope is the most complicated? | The big telescope is the most complicated. |
| Which telescope is less complicated? | The small telescope is less complicated than the big telescope. |
| Which telescope is the least complicated? | The small telescope is the least complicated. |

**9** B:43 **Listen and check (✓). Then ask and answer.**

1 a  b 2 a  b

3 a  b  4 a  b

Which is more beautiful?

The Earth is more beautiful than the moon.

**10**  **Make sentences. Say.**

1 English / complicated / math
2 a thriller / frightening / a musical
3 cats / intelligent / dogs
4 sci-fi movies / interesting / romances
5 big snake / frightening
6 playing video games / important

English is more complicated than math.

**11**  **Read and draw three things.**

1 This one is the most frightening.

2 This one is the least complicated.

3 This one is the most amazing.

**12**  **Read Connor's story. Stick and match the paragraphs to the pictures.**

## The lost spaceship

1 One day in April last year, a spaceship landed in a field. It was only four o'clock in the morning, but the noise and the lights woke Jake up. He looked out of his bedroom window.

2 There was a strange object, like a round spaceship, in the field behind his house. A door opened at the bottom of the spaceship, and some strange people started walking out into the field.

3 They had large heads and small bodies, and they were green. Jake watched with his mouth open. "Am I dreaming?" he said. "Who are those people? Where are they from? What language do they speak?" he wondered. This was more exciting than any dream.

4 He put on his jeans and a T-shirt, went downstairs, opened the front door, and ran to the spaceship. His mom and dad were in bed ....

Connor

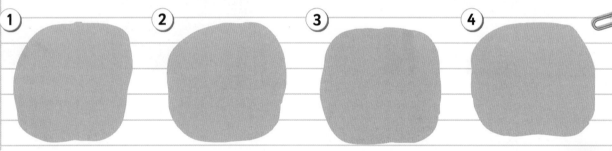

Stick

**13**  **Write questions that Jake could ask the aliens.**

1 Who _____?

2 Where _____?

3 What _____?

4 Why _____?

**14**  **Write the end of Connor's story.**

_____

_____

_____

**15**  Read. Number to match the questions to the answers.

Six space facts!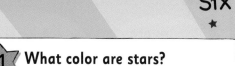

**1** What color are stars?

**2** Who was the first man in space?

**3** When did the first men land on the moon?

**4** Where do astronauts sleep in space?

**5** What happens to your body in space?

**6** Is Saturn nearer to the sun than Jupiter?

a — In 1969, the astronauts Neil Armstrong and Buzz Aldrin were the first men on the moon.

b — You get taller! You can be 5 centimeters taller when you're in space.

c — They can be different colors. Hot stars are blue, cool stars are red, and the sun is yellow.

f — No, it isn't. It's 1,426 million kilometers from the sun and Jupiter is 778 million kilometers from the sun.

d — In sleeping bags. The sleeping bags are on the wall!

e — Yuri Gagarin was the first man in space. He went into space in 1961.

**THINK!**

You want to become an astronaut when you grow up. What should you learn and study? What books would be good to read? Which people and organizations can help you? How can you find out?

**16**  B:45 Listen and check your answers. How many did you know?

MINI-PROJECT Find out about one of the planets from the Internet.

18  **Why are there so many people at the zoo? Discuss your answers.**

**19**  **Circle T = True or F = False.**

1 Champ is the last chimpanzee on Future Island.      T / F

2 Serena goes in the river to the zoo.                 T / F

3 The guards are watching the time machine.            T / F

4 Champ is in a cage on the stage.                     T / F

5 The guards are not near Champ.                       T / F

6 Marta and Chris can't rescue Champ.                  T / F

**20** **Role-play the story.**

**21** **Look at each picture and try to guess what it is. Use your imagination. Then share with a friend.**

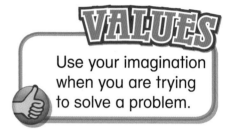

**VALUES**

Use your imagination when you are trying to solve a problem.

| | 1 | 2 | 3 | 4 | 5 |
|---|---|---|---|---|---|
| **Picture** | | | | | |
| **Your guess** | | | | | |
| **Your friend's guess** | | | | | |

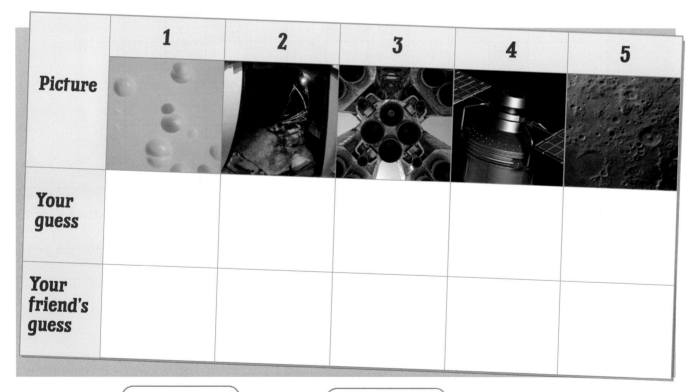

What about Picture 1? Maybe it's a ….

I think, maybe it's a … or a ….

**HOME-SCHOOL LINK**

Tell your family how you used your imagination to solve a problem.    **PARENT**

(22)   **Play. Use space words.**

|   |   |   |   | T¹ | ★ |   | ★ |   |   |   |   |   |
|---|---|---|---|---|---|---|---|---|---|---|---|---|
|   |   |   |   | E³ |   |   |   | ★ |   |   |   |   |
|   |   |   |   | L³ | ★ |   | ★ |   |   |   |   |   |
| S¹ | P³ | A¹ | C⁶ | E¹ |   | ★ |   |   |   |   |   |   |
| ★ |   |   |   | S² |   |   |   |   |   |   |   | ★ |
|   | ★ |   |   | C³ |   |   |   |   |   | ★ |   |   |
|   |   | ★ |   | O¹ |   |   |   |   | ★ |   |   |   |
|   | ★ |   |   | P³ |   |   |   |   |   | ★ |   |   |
| ★ |   |   |   | E² |   |   |   |   |   |   |   | ★ |
|   |   |   |   |   |   | ★ |   |   |   |   |   |   |
|   |   |   |   |   | ★ |   | ★ |   |   |   |   |   |
|   |   |   |   |   | ★ |   |   | ★ |   |   |   |   |
|   |   |   |   |   | ★ |   | ★ |   |   |   |   |   |

| | A | B | C | D | E | F | G | H | I | J | K | L | M |
|---|---|---|---|---|---|---|---|---|---|---|---|---|---|
| **Points** | 1 | 3 | 3 | 4 | 1 | 5 | 3 | 4 | 1 | 8 | 7 | 3 | 5 |
| | N | O | P | Q | R | S | T | U | V | W | X | Y | Z |
| **Points** | 2 | 1 | 3 | 10 | 2 | 1 | 1 | 1 | 5 | 5 | 10 | 5 | 10 |

## How to play

1 Make a word.
2 Write it on the board.
3 Check your points.
4 Write your score.

 = 2 x points for the letter

 = 3 x points for the letter

| | Your words | Your points |
|---|---|---|
| 1 | | |
| 2 | | |
| 3 | | |
| 4 | | |
| 5 | | |
| 6 | | |
| 7 | | |
| 8 | | |
| 9 | | |
| 10 | | |
| | **TOTAL** | |

**23**  **Listen and write.**

| comets | important | spaceships | planet | brilliant |
|--------|-----------|------------|--------|-----------|
| amazing | telescope | complicated | intelligent | frightening |

Last night I was looking at the night sky with my ¹ _____. My dad is
² _____. He helped me set it up because it was a bit ³ _____.
We looked at the moon, many stars, and a ⁴ _____ called Venus. It's
⁵ _____ to see things which are so far away. My dad said that it's very
⁶ _____ not to look directly at the sun with a telescope. So, today I'm
looking at a book about the sun and space. The book has some interesting pictures of
the sun and ⁷ _____. The picture of Saturn's rings is ⁸ _____.
Some people think space is ⁹ _____. They think about going in
¹⁰ _____ and that it may be dangerous, but I think it's very exciting.

**24** **Unscramble and write questions. Then number.**

| 1 I don't know. Do you? | 2 Of course, from Earth! | 3 Well, we can't go by car! |
|---|---|---|
| | 4 That's easy. Yuri Gagarin. | 5 I think it's Mercury. |

**a** in / who / was / man / space / the / first

_____ ☐

**b** nearest / the / sun / what / planet / to / is / the

_____ ☐

**c** get / how / we / to / the / can / moon

_____ ☐

**d** Saturn / why / does / rings / have

_____ ☐

**e** people / where / do / from / come

_____ ☐

**I CAN**   I can ask and answer questions about space. ☐
I can use adjectives to describe and compare things. ☐ 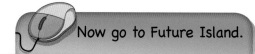 TEACHER

# Wider world 4
## World instruments

1  **Look at photos a–c and make sentences.**

> There's a man playing music.

a

b

2  **Listen and read. Then number.**

**1**

I live in Mali, Africa. Djembe drums are very famous in my country. People made djembe drums more than 1,500 years ago. These drums are made of hard wood and goat's skin. Sometimes there are lovely pictures of animals or people on them, too. We like listening to the djembe drums and dancing. Today, people in Africa play these drums for special celebrations. Famous musicians around the world like playing the djembe drums, too.

Moussa, 11, Mali

**2**

I live in Buenos Aires, Argentina. People in my country play an instrument called the bandoneon. A bandoneon player pushes and pulls on the instrument to make beautiful music. It has square boxes at each end. The boxes are made of wood and have seventy-one buttons on them. Each button can play two different notes. The bandoneon is very difficult to play. It can take ten years to learn. We play the bandoneon when people dance the tango. It's great music for dancing!

Marta, 11, Argentina

c

**3** Circle.

1 Djembe drums are famous in ( Argentina / Mali / Japan ).

2 The boxes on a bandoneon are made of ( metal / glass / wood ).

3 Street singers use the ( shamisen / djembe drum / bandoneon ) to tell stories.

4 A shamisen has ( six / four / three ) strings.

5 People made the first djembe drum ( 40,000 / 1,500 / 2,000 ) years ago.

6 A ( djembe drum / bandoneon / shamisen ) has seventy-one buttons on it.

**4** Ask and answer.

1 What instruments do people play in your country?
2 Can you play an instrument?
3 Which instrument do you want to learn?

3

I'm from Okinawa in Japan. A famous instrument in my country is the shamisen. It's like a guitar. It has a long, thin neck but it only has three strings. People play it with a short piece of wood. Sometimes people sing while they play the shamisen. Street singers use the shamisen to tell stories. People use it in theater, too. Today, some Japanese rock bands also play the shamisen.

Takahiro, 12, Japan

# YOUR TURN!

**Make a list of some instruments and where they're from.**

Djembe drums
– Africa
Shamisen
– …

**Find out about other instruments from around the world.**

**1**  B:49 **Listen and read. Why is Flo sad?**

**1**

It's the last day of camp. I'm sad.

Come on! Let's clean up!

**2**

What are you going to do?

I'm going to collect the garbage.

And I'm going to help Maria.

**3**

I'm going to turn off the lights in the kitchen. Then, I'm going to help Tom.

Yes, I'm going to recycle the bottles.

**4**

Are you going to help, Hannah?

Well, you're all busy .... I'm going to watch!

**2** B:50 **Listen and say.**

**a**

recycle paper

**b**

recycle bottles

**c**

collect garbage

**d**

reuse plastic bags

**e**

turn off the lights

**f**

use public transportation

**3**  **Look at Activity 2. What does your family do?**

**Are you going to recycle paper?**

Yes, I am.
No, I'm not. I'm going to recycle bottles.

**4** **Look at Activity 1. What are they going to do?**

1 Maria and Flo are going to _____.

2 Felipe is _____.

3 Tom _____.

4 Hannah _____.

**5** B:52 **Listen and match. Then say.**

Flo is going to have a big dinner with her family.

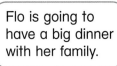

 ①     ②     ③

 ⓐ     ⓑ     ⓒ

**6**  **Look and find. Then say.**

a five things to turn off

b four things to recycle

c five things to clean

I'm going to turn off the TV.

**7** Listen and say. B:53

a

recycle paper /
save trees

b

recycle bottles /
save resources

c

collect garbage /
keep the planet clean

d

reuse plastic bags /
reduce waste

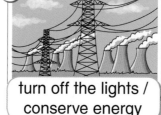

e

turn off the lights /
conserve energy

f

use public transportation /
reduce pollution

**8**  Listen to the song and write. B:54-55

SONG

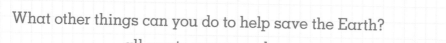

What can you do to help save the Earth?
You can use public transportation and not always take a car.
There'll be less pollution; you can do your part to help save the Earth,
By cleaning up the air, cleaning up the air.

What other things can you do to help save the Earth?
_____ all waste paper, and _____ some trees.
At home _____ the lights, and in stores _____ your bags.
_____ the garbage on the sidewalk.
Keep the planet _____.

So, what's the most beautiful place in the world?
I'm not sure I can say, I really don't know.
The mountains, the oceans, the fields of green.
Let's look after this planet and keep it clean!
Keep it clean, keep it clean.
Let's look after this planet and keep it clean!

**9**  Share your ideas. What can you do to help …?

1 save electricity
2 keep your town clean
3 reduce waste
4 reduce pollution

**LOOK!**
B:56

| What can you do to help? | I can use public transportation. |
|---|---|
| If you reuse plastic bags, you'll reduce waste. | |

**10**  B:57 **Listen and number. Then say.**

1 reduce pollution          2 reduce waste
3 conserve energy          4 save trees
5 save resources           6 keep the planet clean

> If you use public transportation, you'll reduce pollution.

a

b

c

d

e

f

**11**  **Look at Activity 10. Write.**

a If _____, you'll _____.

b _____

c _____

d _____

e _____

f _____

**12** (B:58) **Read. Then number.**

# What are we doing to our planet?

### ① Air pollution

Air pollution has many causes. Factories, cars, trucks, and planes burn fuel and send poisonous gases into the air. These make us sick. Then, in some parts of the planet, large areas of forest are burned every year for farming. The smoke goes into the air, too. We need to use cleaner sources of energy, for example solar energy, wind energy, and the natural force of the water in big rivers.

### ② Global warming

Have you ever been inside a car, parked in the sun? When the windows are closed, it gets hotter and hotter inside the car. The poisonous gases around the Earth are similar to the closed windows in a car. The Earth gets hotter and hotter. This is called global warming. Some scientists think this is changing the climate. In some parts of the Earth it rains a lot; in other parts it doesn't rain for years. This is really bad for all living things on Earth. We must stop poisoning the air!

### ③ Tons of garbage

Billions of tons of garbage are produced by humans every year. Soda cans, plastic bottles, and bags are a big problem. They accumulate on land and in rivers, streams, and oceans, and kill many sea animals. We must reduce the amount of plastic and metal we use, reuse what we can, and recycle the rest.

**a** ▢  **b** ▢  **c** COUGH! COUGH! ▢

**13**  **Match the words to their meaning.**

1 fuel

2 poisonous gases

3 climate

4 accumulate

a the weather an area usually has

b more and more

c something in the air that can make you sick

d something that is burned to get heat or power

**14**  **Read Activity 12 again and underline the solutions to each problem.**

**15** (B:59) **Read. Then number.**

# Our amazing world

a

b

c

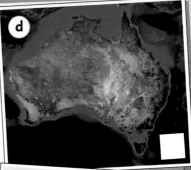

d

e

**1** The highest waterfall in the world is Angel Falls in Venezuela. It's 979 meters high.

**2** Australia is the biggest island and the smallest continent in the world.

**3** The Sahara desert in North Africa is the biggest desert in the world. The Atacama desert in Chile, South America, is probably the driest place in the world.

**4** The Nile in Africa is the longest river in the world but the Amazon river is a very close second. You can see the Nile in nine countries.

**5** Mount Fuji is a very famous volcano in Japan. It's the highest mountain in Japan, too—it's 3,776 meters high.

**16**  **Circle.**

1 The highest waterfall in the world is in ( Japan / Venezuela ).

2 ( The Nile / Mount Fuji ) is in Japan.

3 The Atacama desert is the ( driest / wettest ) place in the world.

4 The biggest island in the world is ( Japan / Australia ).

5 Mount Fuji is ( 3,776 / 979 ) meters high.

6 You can see ( the Nile / the Amazon river ) in nine countries.

**MINI-PROJECT** Find five interesting facts about your country. Write about them and find pictures.

## THINK!

In Brazil, 51 aluminum cans are used per person in a year. Each can weighs 14.5 grams.
**1** How many kilograms of aluminum cans are used, per person in a year?
**2** You want to know the total number of cans that are used in Brazil in a year. What information do you need to calculate this?

**17**  **Listen and read.**

**18**  **Does Zero Zendell know a lot about chimpanzees? Discuss your answers.**

**19** **Circle T = True or F = False.**

1 Zero Zendell eats some ice cream. T / F

2 Zero Zendell knows about chimpanzees. T / F

3 The time machine breaks the cage. T / F

4 Champ likes ice cream. T / F

5 Serena stays in the future. T / F

6 Marta, Chris, and Champ go home in the time machine. T / F

 **20** **Role-play the story.**

Save our planet. Learn to save energy and keep the planet clean.

 **21** **How good are you at protecting our planet? Take the test.**

| Check (✓) the right box. | Never (0) | Sometimes (2) | Always (5) | Score |
|---|---|---|---|---|
| 1 I put my garbage in recycling bins. | | | | |
| 2 I turn off the light when I'm not in my room to save electricity. | | | | |
| 3 I take very quick showers or baths to save water. | | | | |
| 4 I teach my family about recycling. | | | | |
| 5 To save paper, I use my printer only when necessary. | | | | |
| 6 I write on both sides of a sheet of paper when I can. | | | | |
| 7 I don't accept plastic bags at stores. I take my own bag and reuse it. | | | | |
| 8 Some cars and buses pollute the air. I ride a bike or walk when I can. | | | | |
| | | | **Your total score** | |

0–12 points:
You're not helping to save the planet. You must change now!

13–26 points:
You're helping to save the planet, but you can do more! Make an effort!

27–40 points:
Congratulations! You're very good at helping the planet. Keep it up!

**HOME-SCHOOL LINK**

Tell your family about ways to save energy at home.

**22** Play Os and Xs.

I'm going to reuse plastic bags.

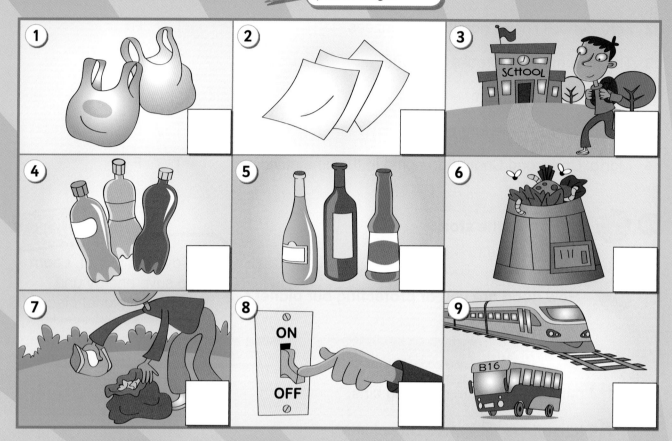

1

2

3  SCHOOL

4

5

6

7

8  ON  OFF

9  B16

 **23** Play Bingo.

recycle paper

reuse plastic bags

walk to school

recycle plastic bottles

collect glass bottles

make compost

collect garbage

turn off the lights

use buses and trains

**24**  **Listen and number. Then write.**

 a   b  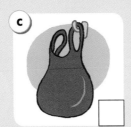 c   d   e

1 You should reuse _____.

2 You can _____.

3 You can _____ and _____.

4 You can _____.

5 You should _____.

**25**  **Unscramble and write. Then match.**

1 bottles / if / recycle / you / the

_____

          a  we'll conserve energy.

2 going / paper / I'm / to / recycle

_____

          b  This will reduce waste.

3 I'm / plastic / going / bags / to / reuse

_____

          c  I'll collect the garbage.

4 the / turn / lights / off / if / we

_____

          d  This will save trees.

5 transportation / if / we / public / use

_____

          e  we'll reduce pollution.

 I can talk about ways to help the environment.
I can talk about what I'm going to do in the future.
 TEACHER

Now go to Future Island.

# Review  Units 7 and 8

**1** Write.

1

_____ is he?

He's an _____.

2

_____ did he go?

He went to the _____.

3

_____ did he go there?

He went by _____.

4

_____ is it?

It's a _____.

**2**  Write. Then ask a friend.

1
_____ is your birthday?

It's on ....

2
_____ do you study English?

I study English because ....

**3** Look and check (✓).

1 Which is more complicated?
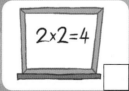

2 Which is less frightening?

3 Which is the least intelligent?

4 Which is the most important?

**4** (B:62) **Listen and order the sentences.**

**a** [ ] Are you going to help?

**b** [ ] OK, you can collect garbage at 3 p.m. Then I'll relax and save my energy.

**c** [ ] I need a break. If you give me fifteen minutes, I'll help later.

**d** [ ] Great. I'm going to sit here and watch!

**e** [ ] I'm going to collect these old newspapers and recycle them.

**5** **Circle.**

**1** If you recycle ( bottles / lights ), you'll save ( transportation / resources ).

**2** If you ( reuse / collect ) garbage, you'll keep the ( energy / planet ) clean.

**3** If you use ( plastic / public ) transportation, you'll reduce ( pollution / resources ).

**4** If you turn ( on / off ) the lights, you'll ( conserve / reuse ) energy.

**5** If you reuse ( plastic / pollution ) bags, you'll reduce ( water / waste ).

**6** If you ( recycle / turn off ) paper, you'll ( reduce / save ) trees.

**6** **Label the picture using the words in the box.**

reuse    recycle    turn off    use

1 _____

2 _____

3 _____

4 _____

**7** **What can you do to help the environment where you live?**

**1** I can _____.

**2** I'm going to _____.

# Goodbye

**1** 🔵 B:63  **Listen and number.**

## The present day

a

c

## The future

b

d

ZERO
ZENDELL'S
ZOO

**2**   **Ask and answer.**

1  What was your favorite scene in the story? Why?
2  Who was your favorite character in the story? Why?
3  What was your favorite song in this book? Can you sing it?
4  Which "*Have Fun!*" page was the best in this book?

**3**  **Which unit are these pictures from?**

a

b

c

d

Unit _____     Unit _____     Unit _____     Unit _____

**4**  **Who said this? Write.**

a "It's there—near the movie theater."          _____  Unit _____

b "Good, I'm really hungry!"          _____  Unit _____

c "… and it made terrible noises …."          _____  Unit _____

d "What are you going to do?"          _____  Unit _____

**5**  **Ask and answer.**

1 What do you think Serena's school is like?
2 Do you want to live on Future Island? Why? / Why not?
3 What type of boy is Chris?

**6**  **What are the good things and bad things about robot dogs and real pet dogs?**

|  | Robot dogs | Real pet dogs |
|---|---|---|
| Good things |  |  |
| Bad things |  |  |

**7**  **Zero Zendell will try to steal more animals. How can you stop him?**

_____

_____

**8**  **Write about your future. Ask a friend to read and comment.**

In the future, I will _____

_____ .

_____

_____

_____

"I've read this."  Friend signs here: _____

Friend's comment: _____

_____

_____

**9** **Choose three friends or family members. Draw and write about them.**

| My _____ | _____ | _____ |
| --- | --- | --- |
| stick photo / draw here | | |

Example: My mom is younger than my dad, but my sister is the youngest.

1 _____

2 _____

3 _____

4 _____

5 _____

6 _____

**10**  **What is a famous food in your country? How do you make it?**
**Draw a comic strip and write.**

| ① | ② |
|---|---|
| ③ | ④ |

1 First, _____

_____.

2 _____

_____

3 _____

_____

4 _____

_____

**11**  **Write four questions. Then ask three friends and write ✓ or ✗.**

| Have you ever …? | Friend 1 Name: _____ | Friend 2 Name: _____ | Friend 3 Name: _____ |
|---|---|---|---|
| 1 been to another country | | | |
| 2 | | | |
| 3 | | | |
| 4 | | | |
| 5 | | | |

**12** **Write words across that fit.**
**Can you find eleven more**
**words in this book?**

F
U
T
U
R
E
I
S
L
S T A R
N
D

# Word list

# Verb list

| Present | Past | Past Participle |
|---|---|---|
| act | acted | acted |
| agree | agreed | agreed |
| be: am/is/are | was/were | been |
| believe | believed | believed |
| beat | beat | beaten |
| blush | blushed | blushed |
| borrow | borrowed | borrowed |
| break | broke | broken |
| bring | brought | brought |
| brush | brushed | brushed |
| build | built | built |
| burn | burned | burned |
| buy | bought | bought |
| call | called | called |
| catch | caught | caught |
| chat | chatted | chatted |
| check | checked | checked |
| choose | chose | chosen |
| clean | cleaned | cleaned |
| climb | climbed | climbed |
| clip | clipped | clipped |

| Present | Past | Past Participle |
|---|---|---|
| close | closed | closed |
| collect | collected | collected |
| comb | combed | combed |
| come | came | come |
| complain | complained | complained |
| complete | completed | completed |
| cost | cost | cost |
| count | counted | counted |
| cry | cried | cried |
| cut | cut | cut |
| dance | danced | danced |
| design | designed | designed |
| dig | dug | dug |
| do | did | done |
| download | downloaded | downloaded |
| draw | drew | drawn |
| dress | dressed | dressed |
| drink | drank | drunk |
| dry | dried | dried |
| dust | dusted | dusted |
| eat | ate | eaten |

| Present | Past | Past Participle |
| --- | --- | --- |
| empty | emptied | emptied |
| explain | explained | explained |
| fail | failed | failed |
| fall | fell | fallen |
| feed | fed | fed |
| feel | felt | felt |
| find | found | found |
| finish | finished | finished |
| fix | fixed | fixed |
| floss | flossed | flossed |
| fly | flew | flown |
| follow | followed | followed |
| forget | forgot | forgotten |
| frown | frowned | frowned |
| get | got | gotten |
| give | gave | given |
| go | went | gone |
| hang | hung | hung |
| has/have | had | had |
| hear | heard | heard |
| help | helped | helped |

| Present | Past | Past Participle |
| --- | --- | --- |
| hide | hid | hid |
| hit | hit | hit |
| install | installed | installed |
| join | joined | joined |
| jump | jumped | jumped |
| know | knew | known |
| laugh | laughed | laughed |
| lean | leaned | leaned |
| learn | learned | learned |
| leave | left | left |
| listen | listened | listened |
| live | lived | lived |
| look | looked | looked |
| lose | lost | lost |
| mail | mailed | mailed |
| make | made | made |
| meet | met | met |
| memorize | memorized | memorized |
| miss | missed | missed |
| mop | mopped | mopped |
| move | moved | moved |

| Present | Past | Past Participle |
|---|---|---|
| open | opened | opened |
| pack | packed | packed |
| paint | painted | painted |
| pass | passed | passed |
| pay | paid | paid |
| photograph | photographed | photographed |
| play | played | played |
| practice | practiced | practiced |
| prepare | prepared | prepared |
| print | printed | printed |
| pull | pulled | pulled |
| pump | pumped | pumped |
| push | pushed | pushed |
| put | put | put |
| rake | raked | raked |
| read | read | read |
| rent | rented | rented |
| rescue | rescued | rescued |
| rest | rested | rested |
| return | returned | returned |
| ride | rode | ridden |

| Present | Past | Past Participle |
|---|---|---|
| ring | rang | rung |
| roast | roasted | roasted |
| run | ran | run |
| say | said | said |
| search | searched | searched |
| see | saw | seen |
| sell | sold | sold |
| send | sent | sent |
| set | set | set |
| shake | shook | shaken |
| shoot | shot | shot |
| show | showed | shown |
| sign | signed | signed |
| sing | sang | sung |
| sit | sit | sit |
| skate | skated | skated |
| sleep | slept | slept |
| solve | solved | solved |
| stay | stayed | stayed |
| study | studied | studied |
| surf | surfed | surfed |

| Present | Past | Past Participle |
| --- | --- | --- |
| sweat | sweated | sweated |
| sweep | swept | swept |
| swim | swam | swum |
| take | took | taken |
| talk | talked | talked |
| tell | told | told |
| text | texted | texted |
| think | thought | thought |
| throw | threw | thrown |
| tidy | tidied | tidied |
| tie | tied | tied |
| touch | touched | touched |
| trade | traded | traded |
| turn | turned | turned |
| use | used | used |
| visit | visited | visited |
| wait | waited | waited |
| walk | walked | walked |
| warm | warmed | warmed |
| wash | washed | washed |
| watch | watched | watched |

| Present | Past | Past Participle |
| --- | --- | --- |
| water | watered | watered |
| wear | wore | worn |
| weed | weeded | weeded |
| whistle | whistled | whistled |
| win | won | won |
| worry | worried | worried |
| wrap | wrapped | wrapped |
| write | wrote | written |
| yawn | yawned | yawned |
| yell | yelled | yelled |

## Acknowledgments

The Publishers would like to thank the following teachers for their suggestions and comments on this course:

Asako Abe
JiEun Ahn
Nubia Isabel Albarracín
José Antonio Aranda Fuentes
Juritza Ardila
María del Carmen Ávila Tapia
Ernestina Baena
Marisela Bautista
Carmen Bautista
Norma Verónica Blanco
Suzette Bradford
Rose Brisbane
María Ernestina Bueno Rodríguez
María del Rosario Camargo Gómez
Maira Cantillo
Betsabé Cárdenas
María Cristina Castañeda
Carol Chen
Carrie Chen
Alice Chio
Tina Cho
Vicky Chung
Marcela Correa
Rosalinda Ponce de Leon
Betty Deng
Rhiannon Doherty
Esther Domínguez
Elizabeth Domínguez
Ren Dongmei
Gerardo Fernández
Catherine Gillis
Lois Gu
SoRa Han
Michelle He
María del Carmen Hernández
Suh Heui
Ryan Hillstead
JoJo Hong
Cindy Huang
Mie Inoue
Chiami Inoue
SoYun Jeong
Verónica Jiménez
Qi Jing
Sunshui Jing
Maiko Kainuma
YoungJin Kang

Chisato Kariya
Yoko Kato
Eriko Kawada
Sanae Kawamoto
Sarah Ker
Sheely Ker
Hyomin Kim
Lee Knight
Akiyo Kumazawa
JinJu Lee
Eunchae Lee
Jin-Yi Lee
Sharlene Liao
Yu Ya Link
Marcela Marluchi
Hilda Martínez Rosal
Alejandro Mateos Chávez
Cristina Medina Gómez
Bertha Elsi Méndez
Luz del Carmen Mercado
Ana Morales
Ana Estela Morales
Zita Morales Cruz
Shinano Murata
Junko Nishikawa
Sawako Ogawa
Ikuko Okada
Hiroko Okuno
Tomomi Owaki
Sayil Palacio Trejo
Rosa Lilia Paniagua
MiSook Park
SeonJeong Park
JoonYong Park
María Eugenia Pastrana
Silvia Santana Paulino
Dulce María Pineda
Rosalinda Ponce de León
Liliana Porras
María Elena Portugal
Yazmín Reyes
Diana Rivas Aguilar
Rosa Rivera Espinoza
Nayelli Guadalupe Rivera Martínez
Araceli Rivero Martínez
David Robin
Angélica Rodríguez

Leticia Santacruz Rodríguez
Silvia Santana Paulino
Kate Sato
Cassie Savoie
Mark Savoie
Yuki Scott
Yoshiko Shimoto
Jeehye Shin
MiYoung Song
Lisa Styles
Laura Sutton
Mayumi Tabuchi
Takako Takagi
Miriam Talonia
Yoshiko Tanaka
María Isabel Tenorio
Chioko Terui
José Francisco Trenado
Yasuko Tsujimoto
Elmer Usaguen
Hiroko Usami
Michael Valentine
José Javier Vargas
Nubia Margot Vargas
Guadalupe Vázquez
Norma Velázquez Gutiérrez
Ruth Marina Venegas
María Martha Villegas Rodríguez
Heidi Wang
Tomiko Watanabe
Jamie Wells
Susan Wu
Junko Yamaguchi
Dai Yang
Judy Yao
Yo Yo
Sally Yu
Mary Zhou
Rose Zhuang

## Unit 1 Adventure camp   page 15

## Unit 3 Where we live   page 37

## Unit 5 Trips page 61

## Unit 5 Trips page 68

- - - - - - - - - - - - - - - - - - - - - - - - - - - - - - - - - - - - - - - - -

## Unit 7 Space page 88